THE LOVE
TREATMENT

THE LOVE TREATMENT

Sexual Intimacy Between
Patients and Psychotherapists

by

Martin Shepard, M.D.

Peter H. Wyden, Inc./Publisher
New York, N.Y.

To
Albert Hofmann
John Lennon
Alan Watts

CONTENTS

PREFACE

Some conventional therapists have told me that it would be a disservice to patients to embark upon the project that resulted in the publication of this book; that the concept of sexual intimacy between therapists and their patients is too threatening for most people who require therapy; that reporting the evidence of such involvements might further encourage unstable therapists toward intimacy with their patients —particularly if it appeared that in some instances such intimacies could be helpful.

I found these arguments specious. For one, nearly every patient is aware of the possibility of such a sexual involvement and has been aware of it since the popularization of the Freudian theory of "transference"—wherein, according to popular legend, the patient falls in love with the therapist. And for those unfamiliar with Freud there have been films and books and off-color jokes that have presented the same possibility.

I also did not feel that patients should be treated like children. I did not feel that they should be "protected" from the harsh realities of life. Such an attitude only prolongs a patient's "illness" by patronizing his or her feelings of fragility.

Further, if such possibilities for intimacy existed and if they could at times be helpful, convention be damned. Honesty requires that we describe what *is*. Therapeutic effectiveness requires that we refine and judiciously use that which is helpful, as opposed to not daring to explore a process that can *also* be abused. As for unstable therapists abusing the process, I would say "forewarned is forearmed." Discussing the uses and abuses of the practice is better insurance of the patient's protection than remaining silent.

M. S.

THE LOVE
TREATMENT

1

THE LAST TABOO

If we want truth, every man ought to be free to say what he thinks without fear. If one side is to be rewarded, and the other punished, truth will not be heard.

Erasmus von Rotterdam

This book represents an attempt to get at the true meaning of sexual intimacy between psychotherapists and their patients. The amount of censure attached to such involvement over the years has clearly prevented truth from being heard. When a relationship is such a constant source of gossip within a profession, and the subject of cartoons and jokes outside it, and when the mass media present it in a critical way, this is persuasive evidence that the practice is both widespread and furtive.

Recently, descriptions of the intimate therapist and his involvements have become less and less fragmentary. Novelist George Bishop gives us a full-length leering view of the extra-professional exploits of his hero/villain in *The Psychiatrist*. And one of 1970's more successful films, *Coming Apart*, dealt with the psychotic deterioration of a psychiatrist who was sexually involved with his patients.

The fact of the matter is that therapist-patient intimacy is not at all uncommon. The extent of the practice will never be

1

fully known because of the combined weight of inner shame and outer censure. Sleeping with your patient—indeed, even daring to discuss the question—represents the last taboo in a field that otherwise prides itself on bringing light into dark places.

One psychoanalyst friend of mine absolutely bridled when I asked him if he had ever been intimate with a patient (although I knew he had had numerous affairs outside of his marriage). He was appalled and insulted that I should even put the question to him. Dr. Harold Greenwald, a clinical psychologist and author, encountered even more forcefully official blindness and unwillingness to deal with the issue. Several years ago, at a meeting of the New York State Psychological Association, he asked whether these involvements should not be studied. "I just raised that question," he told me, "intending, as a clinical psychologist, that it be studied like any other phenomenon. And just for raising the question, some members circulated a petition that I should be expelled from the Psychological Association."

He further adds, "It is one of the great taboos. In a group that I was conducting somebody had spoken about going to bed with a priest and none of the Catholics in the group seemed particularly shocked by that. But then somebody else said that they went to bed with their therapist, and there was a much greater shock. So today that seems like a more immoral act than to go to bed with your priest."

Given the professional reluctance to talk about the practice, how is it possible to be really certain that it is widespread? There are several solid indications that this is so, the first being personal clinical experience. Nearly every therapist has seen patients who have come in complaining about an unhappy prior therapeutic intimate involvement. These complaints are so common that they cannot be dismissed as wholesale fantasies. And occasionally it becomes apparent that the therapists they were involved with were among the most reputable members of the psychotherapeutic community. It is reasonable to suspect, therefore, that a great number of responsible therapists, at some point in their careers, deviate from standard operating procedure and become sexually involved with their charges. They may see several hundred people and only be intimate with two or three. So from the reputable therapist's standpoint, the likelihood of his becoming intimately involved is high. From the patient's point of view, the chance of being intimate with such a therapist is relatively low. It is, however, always a potential reality.

In addition, the findings and views of such authorities as Dr. William H. Masters and Mrs. Virginia E. Johnson must be respected. In their recent book, *Human Sexual Inadequacy,* they pointed out that a sizable number of the nearly eight hundred patients who attended their clinic had had sexual contact with their therapists or counselors. Masters and Johnson raised the question in their book and in subsequent interviews, they said, because "the problem is of such serious import and is encountered with such frequency."

How do they know that the number of these sexual involvements is indeed, as Dr. Masters reported, "quite large"? And that these reports from patients are not based on fantasy?

Dr. Masters conceded that some of his patients may have been fantasizing. But, he said, in many cases "the details are too specific, the presentation is too real, the material is too well supported to be questioned." He concluded: "If only twenty-five per cent of these specific reports are correct, there is still an overwhelming issue confronting professionals in this field."

And I, for one, would not expect a physician who is as highly ranked and widely respected as Dr. Masters to go looking for skeletons in a closet, particularly skeletons that would embarrass his fellow professionals. Not, that is, unless the skeletons are numerous and are rattling so noisily that they should not be ignored.

The rattling increased in the spring of 1970 when one well-known professional journal, *Contemporary Psychoanalysis,* printed an article by a New York psychoanalyst, Dr. Charles Clay Dahlberg, entitled "Sexual Contact between Patient and Therapist." I quote from the opening page:

I have had trouble getting this paper accepted by larger organizations where I had less, but still not inconsiderable influence. I was told that it was too controversial. What a word for a profession which talked about infantile sexuality and incest in Victorian times! Although *controversial* was the word used, it probably was not meant in the usual sense of "disagreement." A friend offered "too hot to handle" as a more likely meaning in this instance. In any case, the object of this paper is to provoke discussion and clarification of the issues involved in a matter that has too long been kept out of the literature.

While Dr. Dahlberg broke ground by getting the subject into the literature, he unfortunately had little first-hand information concerning the nine cases he described, each in a few paragraphs at most.

I quote again:

The most frequent criticism has been that my data on the cases are too sketchy to allow for an adequate understanding of the dynamics and motivations of the therapists as they interlock with the patient's dynamics and motivations. I agree.

And later:

Since these cases reportedly relate in large measure to people who made a complaint, it can be asked: "How many are there who do not complain—who . . . even think they were helped by their therapists' sexual intervention? This is a worthwhile question and could be answered, at least in part.

What I am proposing is a Kinsey-type survey of therapists and patients to probe into the circumstances and results of sexual acting out and near acting out. What was the nature of the interpersonal dynamics when temptation was strong but resisted, and what was the outcome? This would be a tough job, but it could be done.

I am aware of no serious discussion, much less action, on Dr. Dahlberg's proposal for a large-scale survey. At this writing, the situation remains substantially as Dr. Masters has described it: "Despite occasional reports in the psychiatric literature, no real issue has been raised in this exquisitely sensitive area. The time has come."

Today it appears that at last some cracks are developing in the wall that has surrounded the subject and kept it out of realm of serious psychological and sociological discussion. For whatever the difficulties encountered by Dr. Dahlberg in having his article published, the fact remains that he finally did place it in a reputable journal. And whatever problems Dr. Greenwald had when he tried to speak about the subject at a meeting of the New York State Psychological Association several years ago, were rendered ironic indeed in September, 1970. For on the program of the American Psychological Association's annual meeting at Miami was listed a panel discussion entitled "The New Morality in Psychotherapy." At that session, chaired by Dr. Carmi Harari, therapist-patient intimacy consumed so much time that some participants felt that the psychologists were quite "hung up" on this issue.

If the problem was not aired in real depth at this meeting, some of its components were brought into focus. For example, there was no clear-cut answer when one of the panelists asked this question about the use of affection in therapy: "Yes or no? Is it ethical to withhold it?" But at least there was no outcry at the suggestion that, in some situations, a therapist might actually be acting against a patient's best interests if he does *not* become intimate with his charge.

Quite possibly, the relatively tolerant atmosphere at the

convention came about because the discussion made it clear to those present that therapist-patient intimacy is common and that it would be obviously hypocritical not to concede that premise.

"I didn't know there was so much fooling around going on in psychologists' offices these days," one observer at the meeting said.

"Now you know, now you know," said another.

More and more well-known figures are beginning to address themselves to the subject. Dr. William Schutz of Esalen and author of the book *Joy* is on record as having said that a group leader may well be intimate with a group member, provided he does it for the member's good and that he tells the other people in the group about it. It should be noted that he doesn't consider members of such groups to be clinically sick "patients" in any traditional sense. To me, however, that is a mere change of labels and is of no great significance.

Dr. Albert Ellis (and Harold Greenwald was well) distinguishes between patients who are in continuing psychotherapeutic treatment and those who are not in such treatment and attend only occasional marathon or weekend group sessions. Neither of these two psychologists sees anything necessarily wrong in being intimate with a member of the latter category. But both are against intimacy with ongoing patients. Interestingly enough, neither of them objects on moral grounds, but rather for practical reasons. They feel that such involvements tend to inhibit patients from talking to their therapists about their other love affairs (Greenwald) and also that therapists tend to lose their objectivity when sexually involved (Ellis and Greenwald).

Does that mean that a therapist could not be both objective and involved?

"No," said Ellis. "I would say that some therapists could be, but we don't know who they are."

Dr. Masters is one of those most critical of therapist-patient sex: "The greatest negation of professional responsibility is taking sexual advantage of an essentially defenseless patient —but it often happens." But just when does this intimacy constitute taking advantage, and when is it helpful? Until now, nobody has even made a serious attempt to answer this question.

Masters and Johnson themselves have done pioneer work at their Reproductive Biology Research Foundation in St. Louis, Missouri, by treating sexual dysfunctions directly. Not only do they take a standard psychiatric history, instruct on sexual technique, and assign exercises that teach sensory awareness and relaxation, but they have been so bold as to provide surrogate partners for many single men to help them overcome sexual difficulties such as impotence and premature ejaculation. In view of this, I raised the question with Dr. Masters as to why he was so critical of therapist-patient sex. For weren't he and Mrs. Johnson, in effect, having sex with some of their patients—only instead of doing it directly they were once removed by having someone else stand in for them? And couldn't the surrogate partners (one of whom was a woman physician) directly work with certain sex problems without using Masters and Johnson as their brokers, so to speak?

"The difficulty is," said Dr. Masters, "that it's damn hard to be in bed and be objective at the same time. There are very few people who can do this with any success."

Isn't it then, in the final analysis, simply a question of the therapist's integrity that determines whether a sexual experience between a patient and himself will be helpful?

"I don't think that there can't be integrity," he answered. "I only think that it's damn rare. Let's put it this way: of all the therapists, physicians, theologians, and behaviorists that are sleeping with patients every day, certainly not more than five per cent have a great deal of personal integrity involved. In which case it's pretty hard to accept it as a general premise and as a therapeutic approach." Dr. Masters claims to have "blown the whistle" because the needs of the therapist in such cases outweigh those of the patient by ten thousand to one.

I'm not sure that the percentage of disasters is as high as Dr. Masters indicates. For he, and any other therapist, only gets to hear about the failures. People who have been helped through such involvements rarely announce it to future therapists (if, indeed, they ever need a future therapist). In addition, as Dr. Greenwald points out, "when they first talk about it they say how terrible it was. But if I push them, they say that they had only been giving me the expected response. Many; not all. Some experiences really were terrible. But many found that the fact they made it with the therapist reassured them about their desirability."

Still, all the rationales that the aforementioned therapists have given for not having sex with patients are based on prejudiced evidence—the disastrous stories told by people with whom intimacy didn't work out—as opposed to experiences taken from real life at large. But as is obvious, the threat of the law, professional censure, and inner shame combine either to prevent such direct experience or prohibit frank discussion among the therapeutic "sinners" when the event occurs. It is just as Rotterdam said in the fifteenth century: "If one side is . . . punished, truth will not be heard."

And so, a conservative analyst can deliver a paper citing incidents of sexual contact involving *other* therapists and conclude by virtue of theory and second-hand information that such involvements are disastrous. But who has ever seen a round-table discussion of therapists analyzing their *own* "transgressions" in order to understand the meaningfulness of such involvements? For a supposedly scientific field such as psychotherapy, this attitude of "Thou shalt not talk" is absurd.

It is all the more absurd when we consider that many individuals, in the role of friend, lover, or beloved, have had enormous impact on other people, often for the better. Since intimacy can exert profound effects (for better or worse), shouldn't sexual deviations from standard operating procedure in the therapeutic relationship be considered thoughtfully and respectfully? Might not selective intimacy add to our abilities to help people?

I came to the conclusion that the only way to answer this question was to interview former patients who were so involved—and to *seek out* people to interview, as opposed to interviewing people who came into a new therapist's office to complain about a previous one. Not that there aren't complaints in the following accounts; there are many indeed. Yet if a psychiatrist judges therapist-patient sex solely on the basis of cases he sees in his office, he would be on the same shaky ground as if he made pronouncements about marriage solely on the basis of people who came in to see him.

There were other considerations that prompted me to interview patients rather than therapists. First, there was the great reluctance on the part of therapists to acknowledge sexual involvements with patients. Second, I felt that any therapist who did report on the effects of an intimate involvement would have too great a stake in trying to prove the point that the intimacy was beneficial to the patient.

The personal histories that follow are transcribed from taped interviews which I conducted with eleven patients who had been involved in intimacies with their therapists. These people were referred to me by friends and acquaintances whom I had made aware of my interest in the subject.

Every one of the therapists involved in the following ten accounts was well trained by any conventional standards. All either had their Ph.D.'s in clinical psychology or were psychiatrists (M.D.'s who went on to specialize in the field of mental illness). Six of the ten had had additional training and certification as psychoanalysts (although this is not always mentioned in the accounts in order to protect more thoroughly the identities of those involved).

I did not select cases to prove any point. And I conducted no more interviews than are here included. Each interview lasted some two hours. I was mainly interested in finding out how the intimacy came about, what it meant to the patient, how it affected outside relationships (with husband, wife, lovers, friends), how it compared to other nonsexual therapeutic involvements, and what role, if any, sex played in the course of therapy.

These interviews are virtually unedited. My questions— except for the three-way interview with Monica and Gerald —were deleted solely for the sake of readability.

A number of the therapists involved in the following case histories are quite well known and respected within their field. Others have no reputation. Some deserve no respect at all. The reader will be wasting his time should he, however, try to identify the people involved, for all identifying data have been changed: names, locales, physical descriptions, pertinent family data. What does remain are the essentials and actualities of what occurred between patients and therapists.

These cases were not selected for dramatic impact. They do not represent, as far as I can tell on the basis of my informal conversations with numerous therapists, some bizarre, select sampling of what happens when patient and therapist unite. Rather, they represent as unbiased a view of the range and variety of experiences as is possible to obtain at this time without the "Kinsey-type" survey sensibly proposed by Dr. Dahlberg. Both the "mundane" and the "unusual" experiences reported must be judged against the variety of usual and unusual events that occur in the world at large.

This inquiry into patient-therapist sexual involvements was not made in order to condone or condemn the practice. I merely recognized its existence and hoped to find some logical rules or guidelines that would account for good versus bad experiences. And indeed, such guidelines did suggest themselves.

The point might be raised that these accounts are no different from any tale of any affair between two people. I think that that response fails to take into account the special nature of the psychotherapeutic relationship—the respect, trust, and hoped-for cure that the patient brings to the situation.

Intimacy between a patient and therapist is of profoundly more consequence than any ordinary affair, as the reader will shortly discover.

2

THE THERAPIST'S DILEMMA

The dilemma posed by the question of patient-therapist intimacy was first brought home to me as a medical student. A classmate of mine attended a professional meeting that was addressed by a distinguished New York psychoanalyst. The analyst was recalling two separate experiences he had had in treating despondent women. At some point in treatment the first woman demanded that he kiss her. True to his Freudian technique, he attempted to analyze her request. He asked her what she thought her wish meant, he had her relate recent dreams, he explained to her that her feelings for him were really transferred feelings that she had toward significant people in her past—mother or father perhaps—and that they ought to explore this further.

But his efforts were to no avail. In spite of the most diligent analysis, in session after session she repeated her request for a kiss. In addition, she began to threaten that if he did not kiss her she would kill herself. Concerned but unwavering, the analyst told her that "we are here to analyze and not act out" and persisted in his attempts to interpret and understand her request. Following that session his patient committed suicide.

Ten years later the analyst encountered a similar situation.

Again a depressed woman insisted on kissing him and again he persisted in his attempts to analyze this request. When, however, she, too, began to intimate that she would attempt something drastic, he experienced a painful déja vu and, in desperation, consented to a kiss. After leaving his office, she, too, killed herself.

In order to understand properly the box in which psychotherapists find themselves—in order to understand better their anxieties, doubts, and actions—a historical understanding of the psychotherapeutic movement is imperative.

American psychiatry has been heavily influenced by Freudian theory and practice. Quite early in his career, Freud cautioned therapists against treating acquaintances because he felt that a personal relationship tended to interfere with the objectivity and detachment necessary for psychoanalysis.

Psychoanalytic thought presumed that patients were ill because of unresolved situations that existed early in their lives between themselves and their families—needs for love, intense rivalries, great jealousies, and murderous rages. Further, these situations had been so painful to experience that they were repressed—blocked out of awareness—and therefore forgotten by the sufferer. Cure was thought to come about when these repressed (unconscious) thoughts became conscious. The psychoanalyst's role was to decipher the meanings of secret messages thrown up by the unconscious.

His most important tool for accomplishing this was the "transference situation." If he remained impersonal, if the analyst became as much as possible a "blank screen," the patient would *transfer* to him the same attitudes that he had felt toward the significant people in his early life. For instance, if the patient had an overprotective mother who stifled his attempts at independence, there would come a point in treatment where he would endow the analyst with the same over-protective qualities. Further, the patient would harbor toward the therapist the same resentments and expectations that he had held vis-à-vis his mother. The therapist, being neutral, could then demonstrate the unreality of the transferred feelings, get at their origins, and thus presumably cure the patient.

This theory had, of course, a great bearing on the psychotherapist's attitudes toward his patients. In order to remain sufficiently anonymous to receive his patients' projections, he had to restrict radically all contacts with his patients. The therapist went to great pains never to divulge his preferences or life experiences.

"Why do you ask?" was the stock response to any patient who dared ask a personal question.

Chance meetings between therapists and patients were to be avoided like the plague. Most analysts who accidentally came upon a patient at a party would either go out of their way to avoid him or invent some pretext for beating a hasty retreat. Some would not even exchange social greetings at the door on starting or stopping sessions. Others would delay going out of their offices until some ten or fifteen minutes after their last patient had left for the day so as not to meet him accidentally in the elevator, for to the analytically oriented therapist, such contact "ruined the transference."

Somewhere along the line, many therapists began to object to this. Not only was such uncontaminated isolation personally difficult to maintain, but all too many patients failed to respond to it in the hoped-for manner. This was true even when the therapist delivered correct transference interpretations. Typically, orthodox analysts might then claim that there was still more uncovering to be done, that more of the unconscious must be brought to light. Other therapists, however, believed that more than insight and neutrality were required.

Sandor Ferenczi, a great Hungarian analyst and one of the original members of Freud's analytic circle, was one of those who, quite early, was expelled from the inner sanctum because of the heresy of his ideas. He saw nothing wrong with the ancient cure of healing by the laying-on of hands. Indeed, he thought that it was necessary, in certain cases, to supply affectional needs to patients by allowing them to sit in his lap as a baby would, or to offer a warm embrace. And his ideas had profound impact on a later generation of psychotherapists.

These therapists, typified by the late Franz Alexander, argued that patients needed a "corrective emotional experience." They saw their patients as suffering from many of the same childhood dilemmas that the Freudians perceived. But they also felt it was the therapist's task to create a relationship with his patient that balanced the early traumatic one. If, for instance, the father was cold, detached, and autocratic, the therapist attempted to strike a pose of personal sharing and friendly interest. Needless to say, such a therapist replaced the formality of the Freudians with a more relaxed humanness.

Few patients (judging by their complaints) ever seem to have had enough love in their early years. The impulse for a therapist to reach out and touch a lost, suffering, and isolated patient is strong indeed. So, too, is the temptation to make up to patients the love they previously lacked.

Just as there were Freudian cultists on the right who insisted on Olympian detachment, there soon arose cultists on the left who were committed to impassioned involvement. "Love cures" became their slogan and their faith, and sexual intimacies were a standard part of the treatment. One such group in New York had numerous social gatherings to which patients and member therapists came. Not only were these therapists sexually involved with their own patients, but "patient swapping" was regularly practiced. Lest the reader presume that this was a therapist's seventh heaven, I would like to quote an orthodox analyst friend who was inadvertently invited to one of these social gatherings: "For me it was a great disappointment. The room was filled with people who were embracing. But they were all so physically unattractive."

Needless to say, many people failed to respond to this kind of treatment. They could be loved and still suffer. Or they could suck up affection like a sponge and still have a hungering for more. Or they could be used and kept dependent for the therapist's pleasure instead of being helped to become free and independent human beings.

While the believers in intimate involvement tend to shun publicity (societal pressures and professional ethics being what they are), the theoretical underpinnings of their practice are every bit as logical and consistent as those of the sublimely detached. However, theory, whether of the left or right, is only theory. And people, much to the dismay of hypothesizers, rarely allow themselves to be put in boxes; stubbornly they insist upon being treated as unique individuals.

In 1915, Freud took cognizance of the intimate-involvement problem in a paper entitled, "Further Recommendations in the Technique of Psychoanalysis: Observations on Transference Love." He cautioned the therapist against acting on this feeling of attraction for a patient, partly for some of the reasons I have already mentioned and partly because of "conventional morality and professional dignity." He also expressed concern about the effect of sexual acting out on the good name of psychoanalysis among the public. One wonders how much of his suggested caution was in the interest of patients, and how much was in the interest of protecting the reputation of psychoanalysis.

Finally, it should be said that there are cultural reasons why Freud's strictures against intimate involvement need not necessarily apply today. America in the 1970s is hardly the same as Vienna at the turn of the century. A sexual revolution is occurring in this country, if indeed it has not already succeeded. It is no longer imperative to marry, or even love, a person with whom one is intimate. Sexual fulfillment for its own sake is taken for granted by many as a natural right.

While most professional therapists are years behind this revolution (how could they not be when they were raised in an earlier generation?), there nevertheless exist more options for them than ever before in the ways they can relate to patients. While a sexual response from a therapist in the 1930s might have badly shocked a patient, such a move in the 1970s would be taken in stride by many.

This is not to argue for indiscriminate intimacy. In many circumstances, intimacy between therapist and patient can be downright harmful, as several of the accounts in this book show. But it can also be enabling, rewarding, and productive of growth. I have no theoretical position to defend. I only wish to examine the uniqueness of whatever it may be that two particular individuals—a patient and a therapist—bring to their sexual involvement.

3

A CONFESSION

While I was a psychiatric resident, I treated an attractive adolescent lesbian who was hospitalized after having made numerous attempts to commit suicide. Her depression was directly related to the shame she felt about her homosexuality. When she was able to share this secret with her mother, the intense shame lifted, along with her severe depression. I lost track of her after that because she transferred to another hospital for further care.

Some years later, while engaged in private practice, I was surprised to hear from her again. She wanted to see me to discuss some problems she was having. One of them had to do with the type of work she was doing and quickly resolved itself. The other involved her unsuccessful attempts to achieve heterosexual satisfaction in spite of many years of analytically oriented work on the problem.

As far as I was concerned, she was one of those painfully shy and fearful souls who slipped into active homosexuality accidentally. While at a party in her early teens she became quite drunk and passed out in a bathroom. She was there revived and seduced by a somewhat older lesbian friend. She knew that the physical contact between them was pleasurable, and she passively continued in this relationship. Had a boy gently seduced her at the same impressionable age and in the same inebriated state, I am certain she would have been heterosexually content. But that was not to be her fate.

While she found herself attracted to men, she was most fearful of being penetrated. And of course she did not talk about her homoesexual satisfactions or her fears of penetration with her male dates.

And so, while she would go out on dates, her fearfulness was such that it would have required a man with the wisdom of a sage and the patience of a saint to be able to figure out what she wanted and to fulfill her wishes in a nonthreatening way. She might have managed heterosexuality if a man had only touched her on the ankle one day, her knee the next month, her thigh the month after, and her vagina still later. And still, if at the point of penetration she had said, "Wait, not yet," he would have had to be prepared to wait. Such a selfless man had been impossible for her to find. Yet finding such a person seemed essential if she was to experience the pleasures of heterosexuality.

So here was I, her therapist, supposedly dedicated to helping her to achieve her goal, watching her flounder about futilely. And to make it all the worse, I felt that I could easily do for her what her dates wouldn't.

For one thing, she made her dilemma intelligible to me. For another, I found her attractive enough to know that I could respond adequately. Also, my love life and sex life were fulfilling enough to allow me to abstain patiently when she became frightened. I was convinced that for me to offer myself to her this way was clearly the most therapeutic thing I could do.

But I did nothing of the sort. I didn't even mention the possibility.

"It's crazy," I thought. "She'd be shocked." But I think that these were mere rationalizations for my more basic fears: "Suppose she tells someone?" . . . "What would my colleagues think of me?" . . . "I'd be disgraced."

And so, I *knew* that I failed to do the right thing at the right time. I *knew* it even if all my fellow therapists told me that my abstinence was ethical. I *knew* I was wrong to withold this offer, even if other professionals told me that such an involvement would have been a manifestation of my own neurosis, my own "counter-transference," my own *transferring* onto her my secret agendas, misperceptions, and inappropriate responses that arose out of my own needs and hangups.

I *knew* that it was my own conventionality, sexual shame (the feeling that it's all right to relate to a patient verbally, but somehow "dirty" to do so physically), and my desire to protect my professional credibility, that kept me from taking the properly helpful, if unorthodox, step.

I would hope that my concern with my reputation does not interfere with my therapeutic effectiveness again.

4

BEVERLY

"You can't always get what you want"

Beverly is an editor. She lives in a suburb of a large Midwestern city. A still very handsome woman at forty-nine, she wears a tan-and-brown patterned silk print dress, which in clinging to her body reveals her full-bosomed shapeliness. Her red hair has been cut and dyed with care and sophistication. Her legs could be those of a woman twenty years younger. Her voice is deep, sure, and well controlled. Her face is lined. Her lips are full.

The over-all impression she gives is one of worldliness and graceful elegance.

Her account in her own words follows.

My first therapist was a very eminent therapist by the name of Louis —. It was really just therapy in conversation and it didn't work. I had a lot of anger and a lot of hostility and a lot of sexual aggression. I felt I was the most attractive woman to anyone. I went to see him just because I was miserable. I wanted to get divorced. I was twenty-eight years old and I hadn't had any children and I was dissatisfied with my husband and I wanted to leave him. I was working and I wanted to do interesting things, writing, and I was just completely unsettled.

I didn't have the courage to leave my husband. It was a combination of my family having very high standards and very little money. I was afraid to leave my husband because I was afraid of being economically dependent upon my parents, and I didn't want to be economically dependent upon myself. I was afraid to take that responsibility. My sister, who is seven years older than myself, was then and still is unmarried. I was afraid that if I left I would somehow, like my sister, get into my mother's clutches again. Only by marrying had I separated myself from this woman. So I went to Louis and for all the eminence that he had, he really had no more understanding of me than if I'd been talking to that picture on the wall.

I'd come in and he'd say, "Oh, you're so attractive and so charming and so intelligent, why don't you utilize your anger and aggression." All words. It never got beyond an outer layer of feeling. Anyhow, he said to me (and I'll never forget this), "The birds and the bees mate. Why don't you have children?" At this point I really didn't know what I was doing, but it seemed an appropriate time and I went ahead and had child number one.

I was seeing my therapist three times a week, but it was not real analysis as I was seeing him face to face. He was one of the first analysts to have his patients sit up. I never was able even to express my anger about him. He was a skinny little man and I never could tell him that—that I thought he was sort of awful, physically. In the meantime I went to him for maybe two or three years. I had the child and nothing much happened.

I had a lot of sexuality and a lot of sexual aggressiveness that was not coming out with Louis, and I didn't know how to use it at all. I was attracted to other men constantly but I always kept it to myself. Sometimes I'd almost come to it and play with somebody, but I kept myself in check. I was still faithful to my husband.

I had lots of dates when I was in college and my idea was to be the most sought-after and popular girl. Seven guys a night would call me for dates. Yet my moral code was such that I remained a virgin. As a matter of fact, that was how I came to marry Al.

While I was dating Al I was also seeing another man that I was terribly in love with. He wanted to be intimate with me, but I insisted on marriage first. Since he wasn't prepared to marry, nor I to be intimate without it, he stopped seeing me. And on the rebound I married Al. I didn't love him when I married him, and from the beginning I found myself attracted to and flirting with other men. But I didn't let myself have a complete sexual relationship.

Then I had a second child. And I remember this complete misery. I wanted success and I dreamt up an idea for a column and I wrote up this column and it almost got into sixty-four newspapers. But then I pulled back on it. Any time I was going to have this big New York kind of success I pulled away from it. Then I remember, after the second child was born, just getting in the car and driving around, full of a kind of misery that I didn't understand, just amorphous. At the same time my exterior life was good and nobody knew this. I was a wife, and busy, and working part-time along with raising the kids.

So then I got therapist number two who was Elaine —, a woman therapist, whom a friend recommended. I went to her once or twice a week for a year. Again nothing happened at all. Just this terrible anger and aggression and misery. So finally she suggested I go see a male analyst who was a friend of hers. I said I really didn't want to, but she sent me there anyway. I was still very bottled up, unhappy with, but faithful to my husband, and I really wanted a big New York success. That was the dream and fantasy of my life. I see now that to get it you have to be single-minded and directed and I just wasn't able to do that. And I was unhappy because my husband wasn't making enough money. That was the other thing.

I wanted big money—a big house, et cetera. So she sent me to
see this Robert —.

I went to see him once and I knew he was my type physically. One of my things all through my life was to be very
seductive in terms of a man. I enjoyed the role that everybody
wanted to sleep with me and it was just fun. I loved the attrac-
tiveness and it was just great. Finally, in my middle age, I've
gotten to the point where I know it isn't going to happen that
often and I'm used to it. But up to about five years ago it was
central in my life, and I wasted too much God-fucking time
on it, which really kept me from other things.

When I saw him he had the same kind of rugged face as my
father. A Jewish rugged face with a large rawboned nose,
very tall.

I was then thirty-three. I had been married for eleven years.
He was an eminent forty-year-old married psychoanalyst. He
was extremely good-looking, and immediately I was turned
on. But I could see that he was reacting to me in a way that
wasn't professional.

Of course in those days I was very innocent about therapy.
Therapists seemed like gods. They were way on top and I was
a lowly human down here at the bottom. But I called Elaine
and I said, "It just doesn't feel right. I think he likes me."
And she said, "Ohhff! You're manufacturing this." Anyway,
but the fifth visit he fucked me. But, you know, it wasn't very
good sex.

When I first went in to see him my complaints (as always)
were a tremendous tension in the body that was never quite
relieved by sexuality and my general malaise with life—depression, hating the female role, hating the house thing,
wanted a big career, still taking care of the kids, disliking my
husband, who was a very cold man, all the middle- and upper-
middle-class symptoms that were so crummy in a way. As I
look back, it was just crummy, and immature, and just a
complete inability at the age of thirty-three to really handle

life at all. You know, *expecting everything to be mine.* Thinking that I was the Princess (or the Duchess—as they used to call me—) and that it would all come my way.

I could tell from the start that he was attracted to me. And two or three times I went back to discuss it and I'd say, "I really like you. I want you to sleep with me. I want an affair with you."

When I first told him that, he just put it off and treated it like a professional thing, saying, "This is part of the problem. Let's analyze it," and so forth. Then the last time I went in to see him, the fifth time, he wasn't seated in his office. He was seated in the waiting room, slouched in the chair in a completely unprofessional manner. I reached over and kissed him, because it was appropriate at that moment in the terms of the way he was sitting there. It seemed a come-on. He had changed. He didn't greet me standing up. He wasn't sitting in his office, but in the waiting room and leaning back.

I was very seductive, extremely attractive, and I think he was probably at a bad point in his marriage. I suspect that I flattered him enough and he was attracted to me enough so that by the fifth visit, instead of analyzing it, he was receptive.

So the affair started. He took me into his office and, I'm trying to remember now (this I don't remember and I've blocked out) whether the first time we had regular sex. Because for the entire six and a half years thereafter, most of the sex—most of the time—consisted of my satisfying him orally. Sometimes he would satisfy me. Sometimes it would be joint fellatio and cunnilingus. Many times I did not have an orgasm.

He came too quickly and he didn't really satisfy me. I have to say right off that he suffered from premature ejaculation for most of the nearly seven years I saw him. But we never talked about that. It took me so long to come to myself that it's only been in recent years that I've been able to discuss sexuality—and not with him at all. Because in all the years I had the relationship with him, I still had him somewhat on a pedestal.

I had a fantasy he would marry me, even though he said he would never leave his wife. I thought maybe he would. And I wanted him desperately. And it would have been (in terms of the odds and in terms of the circles we moved in) a very legitimate marriage. In other words, it wasn't a fantasy that was way out. We belonged to the same kind of social level and intellectual level and so forth. So all that could have been possible. And I remember hearing at the time of someone else in the city, another well-known analyst, who had married a patient. This was the big scandal of the time. So I thought, "Well, maybe it could happen to me too."

I only saw him five times as a patient. Then he sent me the bill. The bill went through his stenographer. I never forgot this. He said, "You don't have to pay it"—I can't explain it, it was almost as though he said, "You don't *have* to, but if you want to it's okay." Horrible.

So I really wanted this guy. And it was the beginning of knowing in my life that I was never going to get what I really wanted. I'd say that was when my life started in another way.

Strangely enough, he lived about six or seven blocks away from me. I worked in town at that time, even though my kids were little, three days a week. He used to come by often (my husband left for work very early) and take me to work in the mornings. And in the afternoons sometimes I'd go to his office and I'd get a ride home. And then we'd have sex very briefly. So that I would see him then several times a week for several years. But I never knew how to really let him know my longings.

And I was so immature. Somehow, just the fact that I had even a tiny piece of this great god (who did not talk very much—he was a nonverbal person) was almost enough.

Physically he radiated a good deal of strength to me. Because he was about six feet, three—or four. And he seemed to have (seemed to, I say in quotes) a kind of compassion or understanding that my husband didn't have. He was also an analyst, which I thought at that time was absolutely great. An analyst today is nothing more than a truck driver if he isn't a person. But at that point—you have to understand what was going on in analysis at that time—this seemed to me like a coup. I had done a great thing. I had captured an analyst. I had gotten him from his pedestal, so that was enough to sustain me. And I felt young enough and gay enough and attractive enough to feel that somehow this could go on forever. Or that it would come to fruition. I was enjoying the double life and it was kind of fun and exciting. I was attending a lot of parties (not with him) and I had an interesting job. I spent about seventy per cent of my time, though, fantasizing about this man. Even when I was working. He really had me. That's all I can say.

From his end, all that he would ever say to me was that I gave a lot and that I helped him tremendously and that I meant a great deal to him. Other than that he never really expressed his feelings. The only time that I ever heard from him in a letter was once when he was traveling in Europe with his wife and I got a hastily scrawled note from somewhere in Hungary: "I can hardly wait to get back to you. I miss you very much." And in those six and a half years we only had dinner together twice. Because we lived in a small town. He'd be seen with me. And once I think I left my gloves in his car and his wife found them. And I think he said once he was furious because someone had told his wife we were having an affair, which he had vigorously denied.

He told me many times that he never intended to give up his marriage; that life consisted of trying to stay on the fence, and when you fell off, you did. Meaning, you know, when you couldn't contain yourself any longer you had an affair.

My husband really knew all along that I was seeing Bob.

As a matter of fact, at about the time I began this affair with Bob I also began one with another man who was very important to me. But Al was having his own affair so we just accepted it, like stupid kids.

Bob told me not to divorce Al. He said, "I don't see why you're getting divorced." I got divorced when I was forty. My husband was in the shoe-manufacturing business and he moved his business down South and I went with him for a year. And I've often wondered whether part of leaving my husband in the South was somehow to get back in the city with Bob. I would write him long letters, to which he'd never reply in writing, or I'd call him on the phone. During that year I called him a couple of times in order to help myself stick it out. But after a year of living in the South, when it didn't work out with my husband (because I didn't want it to, and I didn't like it down there, and the relationship became more stark in that setting than it was in the Midwest), I came back and got my divorce.

I went to see Bob a few times and I said, "I don't want any sex, I just want your help." But somehow before a couple of hours were over the sex would come about. And I felt used— badly used. I wanted his help as a man, or like a father, but he would turn it into a sexual encounter. And I couldn't say "No," because I never had that power. I couldn't with him, anyway.

He tried to help me, anyway. I needed a job at that point. I had done some editing before, and he said he would call someone for me. But I called him later and I said, "I don't want your help. I don't want your contact." So I never pursued the contact that he was willing to make for me.

After that I kept having affair after affair with all kinds of men. A black guy and then an orgy and I just went through the gamut, because I had no solidity in my life, no base. But on the outside I was still living in a house and bringing up the kids and trying to earn some money. It was very bad. Now that I look back on it it would have been a good experience if I had had some kind of base from which I was operating. It was sort of necessary for me to expunge all this stuff from my soul. To see what it was all about sexually. But it wasn't necessary to leave my husband to do it.

After the affair with Bob began I laid off therapy for several years for the first time. But then I wanted to get rid of Bob and I couldn't get rid of him. I wanted to stop the relationship but I couldn't do it—it was like being an alcoholic, it was obsessive to me. So I went to another therapist, who was a friend of his, to see if I could break it off. Bob didn't really like that. He didn't like it because this other therapist evidently told a few people, and it got around the little therapeutic community in this little world. Bob told me that he was furious at the other therapist for having mentioned it because Bob—this is an important point—Bob whitewashed the thing to an extent, saying that I was never in therapy with him. That was his line, because I had only come the five times.

But I never would have met the man. I mean, I could have gone from that day to this, and even though I knew who he was, I never would have met him if it hadn't been for the therapy.

Seeing Bob's friend never really helped me break off with Bob. He was an awful man, really, and I regret the dough that I wasted on him. I regret psychoanalysis in general, which I think is a crock of shit, most of it. I saw this guy a couple of times a week for a couple of years. But it was just words again. I do remember one thing that he said to me; "You treat your body like a piece of raw meat." I remembered it well but I was unable to act on it. He tried to rid me of the obsession of giving my body so casually. And maybe at this point I did see Bob less, but I never really severed the relationship. And even though I didn't see him so much then, he was still always there. He was there in my mind and there to call.

Bob never tried to turn me against my husband. He tried to

make me understand. I remember one day we were driving home. He was very taciturn and didn't always express himself much, and he just looked at the sky and looked at the grass and he said, "This is all there is. The sooner you realize it, the better." But, you know, it took me until I was about forty-five years old to recognize that simple thing emotionally. Nobody could tell me. Because I wanted to grasp all of life.

Now I finally see the Zen thing—the more you grasp, the less you get. Bob was a wise man. He was able to deal with his affair. He knew it was something out here. But I don't think he realized the depths to which it plummeted me. Or if he did, he preferred to draw a curtain. Perhaps he should have cut me off, but I don't know how I would have reacted then. He was like a savior, a guardian. It was what really kept me going for years. I used to think, "I'll go from year to year; I'll take it as it comes." I needed some kind of solidity in my life which I really didn't have, and I guess he provided that.

About five years ago, shortly before I met the guy I go with now, a warm, nice guy, I just seemed to absolutely collapse. I went to Europe on a vacation and I went back to the hotel room and I just sat there and cried. I think it was partly an early menopause. I was just very depressed. I couldn't move. I was the only woman editor at a large and important publication and I was running like mad—in addition to the two kids and all the dates. I was just absolutely going to collapse.

And so when I got back, this friend of mine who was a therapist and lived nearby said, "Why don't you see this friend of mine who has a new technique of visual imagery. Maybe he can help you."

Anyway his visual-imagery techniques seemed to really help me. I put together scenes out of the past. Like he'd say, "See the mother and father in the living room, and you're the child—like on a little TV set—with them, and see what happens." After a while the images would begin to move by themselves and the child winds up striking the father, running to the mother—a whole series of pictures in my life taking place. Anyway, all I can say to you is that out of all the therapy I've ever had, I feel more at oneness and more at peace with myself from that than from anything else that's ever happened to me.

I'm not bitter about Bob. I don't think I would have been able to do things any differently, I really don't. It was a necessary thing to go through, I think. As I grew up he was the kind of a man I would like to have married. A man who came from a poor background and had made his way and had a sense of realism about life, which my ex-husband didn't have. My husband came from a protected, rich environment and he's still a kind of shit—he doesn't care about seeing my son, you know. So what can I say? I'm not one to go back. I'm not one to say that I could have done it differently.

The good things about the affair with Bob were that it gave me six and a half years of a sense of stability. It gave me someone to count on that I respected and liked in many ways. It gave me a sense of power, having this extra relationship in my life. And we talked of many things as we drove to and from town three times a week for six and a half years. I liked him.

The bad thing that really sticks out in my mind was the sexual thing, because it was really so unsatisfying to me. He was really a lousy sexual partner. Under any circumstances. I've had so many sexual partners since then that I know he was lousy. When I look now, in my mind, I see the image of myself sucking him. I see that the sex, when he did enter me, wasn't satisfying to me because he came so quickly. And what I'd say to myself was, "You! You're the big analyst. You're telling other people how to handle their sex lives and you are suffering from a form of impotency." It was like a private little secret that I knew. And one year, he was the president of the local analytic chapter, he was the big man on campus. But he always would say to me, "I'm not like this with my wife." And you know what? I think that's a crock of shit.

So I didn't really stay with him for sexual reasons. It was the stability and it was somebody to talk to, someone outside my marriage. And I think he cared for me—he really did. I think even now, if I would call him tomorrow and say, "Bob, I need to see you," he'd say, "Come over," immediately.

Another bad thing was that in a sense, it prolonged my sense of fantasy about life. Because somewhere in the back of my mind I did think that I would get him. I didn't know how. I had no plan for getting him. But I felt somehow it would come to fruition. He would be mine. Because that's the way my life operated. I might have gotten disillusioned quicker. But I saw other things work out. Like with a friend, Ellen. Her affair worked out, and after many years she and her lover divorced their spouses and married one another. So I'd seen other people have this thing that turned out. And mine just didn't.

I used to feel that our affair was really a destructive thing. Very destructive. I couldn't stay away from him and we were not really going anywhere. But I guess in retrospect Bob was responsible for catalyzing a lot of changes in my life—although it's taken me about twelve years to see it.

It was less than a month ago that I related the story of this affair to a friend of mine. He said that it sounded to him as though it began a series of disillusionments for me that were eventually helpful to me. I stopped being a princess. I became more responsible for myself. I became more sexually fulfilled, although not with Bob. I do know that I'm probably in the best position that I've ever been in in my life, right now.

I guess, in a sense, through talking about it recently, I've got a new perspective on the relationship. Now I'd rate it over the fifty per-cent mark in terms of positive experience. Before, in the general ambiance of my feelings, it was only a negative experience. So I learned something.

AUTHOR'S POSTSCRIPT

The initiative toward an intimate relationship in this instance clearly came from Beverly. She made the initial suggestions and the initial advance, and it really made no difference whether Bob was sitting in his office or his waiting room.

At the start of the affair, Beverly was clearly still getting what she wanted. As the "Duchess," her expectations were that everything would come her way. Events in her life were judged according to whether or not they lived up to her fantasies. If the fantasies were gratified, she had "positive" experiences. If not, the experiences were "destructive."

Insofar as her dream of marrying Bob never materialized, she had felt their affair to be harmful. Yet, as she said, "It was the beginning of knowing in my life that I was never going to get what I really wanted."

Is this to be taken as a statement of personal inadequacy, failure, or hopeless resignation? I think not. Indeed, after seeing her last therapist she felt "more at oneness and more at peace with myself than from anything else that's ever happened to me." So I would translate her statement to read, "It was the beginning of knowing in my life that I was not the center of the universe—that all of my deep desires would not necessarily materialize, because other people were not necessarily at my command."

And this awareness—the awareness of one's limitations—I would deem to be valid and useful and therapeutic.

While Beverly's official therapy ceased after their affair began, it is interesting to note that their three-times-a-week meetings continued in car rides and conversations to and from work. Bob seems to have been very straightforward with her and did not lead her astray about any possibility of marrying her. Had he been more therapeutic, he might have actually raised the question of what she was hoping to get out of the relationship—why she continued it when he was a poor lover and offered no prospects of marriage.

Had he done this, Beverly might have disillusioned herself more rapidly of the notion that she was a princess.

5

KATHY

"He made me feel like a natural woman"

A case worker at a social-service agency, she has eyes that are dark and flashing behind "schoolmarm" glasses. She wears black pants and a shiny black sweater. Her legs are folded beneath her as she sits snuggled up in an oversized armchair. Her blonde hair falls down to her shoulders. She is a flirtatious twenty-three.

When I was fourteen I first went into therapy because I was not, so to speak, functioning. I was only getting C's in school in spite of constant studying. Somehow the material just didn't sink in. And I was subtly rebelling against my parents and worrying them with my depression.

I was really very unhappy. One day my mother said she had met someone, and because I was so unhappy I might want to speak to that person.

So I saw this lady therapist for three years until I went off to college. Her name was Jane. It was a very superficial kind of therapy. I never got any rage out. I never cried, I never expressed my real anger. I never felt good when I left her office. I couldn't get over that. I couldn't understand why I'd go for therapy and feel so shitty when I'd leave all the time. It just seemed really weird.

I went back into therapy three months after I was married. I was twenty-two then. I was fighting violently with my husband and I was very frightened. I felt I needed to go for help someplace and I didn't know where to go. I went back to this woman and she directed me finally (because we couldn't make it) to the woman I'm in therapy with now. Frieda.

I was again very unhappy. My husband and I were fighting and screaming. Things weren't just what they were supposed to pan out to be. My husband hit me, which really got to me. He'd push me around and he was always putting me down, telling me what a nothing I was, that I was just a case worker. And making fun of case workers. And all he was was a lousy graduate student. What a shit to pull that on me! So I guess that's more or less why I went in.

After I went into therapy with Frieda (who I've really been happy with) there were other discontents. I had to give all my money to my husband. Like, I was supporting him so I couldn't buy anything for myself.

I couldn't believe that Richard (my husband) could be so mean that he'd want to hurt me. And physically hurt me. Not just emotionally. And I mean he really would sock it to me. It was unbelievable. And I had no defenses for that. I didn't expect that. That he would be that way.

I first met my husband when I was sixteen years old. He was very good for me then. I guess we should have let go of each other but we didn't. I married him because I wanted to get out of my house and I felt I loved him (I still think I may in some peculiar, odd, crazy kind of way). I certainly had a sense of some kind of dependency on him. I felt I loved him but it was like role playing. I remember, when I was a little girl—it's funny—my grandfather used to call me a prima donna. And like I thought I was just going to be one of those.

Well, shortly after the marriage began, my fantasy of what it would be like just came crashing in on me one day. It just wasn't going to be the way I wanted it to be. I thought I would really love housekeeping, but I hated it. I don't do any of it now. I remember getting on my hands and knees and scrubbing a bathroom floor and then coming to the realization that it's crazy—that I had really thought I was going to enjoy this. It was ludicrous to fool myself into thinking that I would. I had this whole fantasy in my mind that everything was going to be beautiful, that we would communicate with each other and understand each other.

At the time when I went into therapy there was no reason for Richard to be doing what he was doing to me. Because I was still in the bag of wanting to please him. I was doing everything his way. I was denying myself, but everything I did was wrong anyway. Like the meals I made. It wasn't the typical complaint that I'm a lousy cook, but like I didn't give him enough to eat, or there weren't the things that he wanted in the house. And that would get to me. Stupid things. But they would hurt me. They really would hurt me. I don't remember what would provoke him to punch me.

After I was in therapy for a year, I went to a marathon* run by this psychologist, Adele —. It was very frightening and very powerful. Very overwhelming. I was scared to death. There was an outpouring of all these emotions and feelings and so on. But it opened me up, because I was a very tight, very closed person. I couldn't scream and I couldn't raise my voice. So this was like a beginning. But I had trouble going back. I couldn't go to another marathon for a year.

In the next year my husband and I grew more and more distant. I was showing my anger and my rage. I was beginning to fight back. And I was feeling very cheated as a woman. He didn't make me feel like a woman, I think—or fully like a woman. Like I wasn't enjoyable to him.

* A marathon is a therapeutic group that runs without interruption for an extended period of time—most often between twelve and twenty-four hours. Intense experiences occur with frequency in such groups because the constant interactions with others cannot be readily broken off. Also the defenses of the participants are worn down over such a protracted time span.

My husband was the only one I had sex with before I was married. I was tempted with others but I never really did. I played little games with men sometimes, but I was frightened of sex and my own sexuality and sensuality. So he was the only one.

There was another guy, Tom. I dated him when we were adolescents and I more or less have an affair with him now. It began a few months after Adele's marathon. I came home one day and I called him. We met, and we sat, for about two and a half hours. I hadn't seen him or spoken to him since I married and it was a very emotional kind of meeting. I was very turned on to him. And then I'd see him when he'd come in to the city once a month from out of town. Later he'd come in more often.

Tom really began to make me feel more like a woman, although sexually I wasn't really that satisfied with him for a long time either, although it was better than what I was having with my husband.

While I could have orgasms with Richard, I wanted more. I'd have fantasies of wanting to be licked all over but there were things he wouldn't do. I mean he'd play with my clitoris and lick me but it really wasn't even an enjoyable kind of thing. It was almost like something he had to do to arouse me but nothing he got pleasure out of. It was all very controlled —held in tight. It was hard for me in those circumstances to abandon my control. I tried. But it was very difficult. He'd stop me—he'd push me away when I'd play with his penis or suck it.

He'd say he really liked it, but he was always pushing me away saying, "You're exciting me too much . . . don't go so fast, don't go so fast." Or he'd lie there all of a sudden in the middle of play and he'd stop and have a cigarette and he'd want me to keep playing with him. It was this whole fantasy I felt he was into where I was a slave to him. Like I was his wife, and I was supposed to be home to make him dinner and do this for him and do that for him and it was a very one way kind of deal.

Then I met Jason.

Things were going so badly that I was thinking of divorcing Richard. And then my analyst Frieda came around and suggested I go to another marathon being given by Jason — and I said I'd go.

Everyone idolized Jason. It was just an unbelievable kind of thing, like he really was God. Like he was the greatest. The world's greatest analyst. This occurred last summer. It seems like years ago.

Jason was a married man of sixty-one—older than my father. I was very nervous and shaking. There were also many more people at this marathon than there were at the other one, which was sort of frightening. But I think within two hours I really got into it. I got into a physical battle with a guy. And Jason came on top of me and started to kiss me. I think this involved my brother—this point—this encounter I was involved in with this guy, this physical thing. I was becoming aware of my sexuality towards my brother at that time also and I was really turned on to my brother.

And I pushed Jason away (who was psychodramatizing my brother) and said I didn't want him anymore as I had come to a resolution kind of thing with this encounter. And during the break he came over to me and he said that he thought I was amazing; that I got into things very quickly and I could go extremely deep and very freely, and would I be interested in doing a demonstration with him at a convention? I sort of felt excited, like, "Gee, he thinks I'm great," or something. So I really dug it, but I sort of left it where it was.

I had very warm feelings towards Jason. I think that was the only physical kind of thing. I think we did hug each other and kiss each other at the end of the marathon, and there was a great deal of warmth as there does exist at the end of most marathons. And I was very turned on to him. I remember going back to my therapist and saying how great he was. The marathon had been very successful for me. I had explored a lot of relationships in terms of my father. I had been very sick as a child and I had been able to role-play the drama of my operation. I was born with a congenital intestinal obstruction and I felt that in operating on me, they had removed all my female organs, and that I wasn't a woman, and that I really had been brutalized by doctors. Have you ever been man-handled and torn apart? I had fantasies about being ripped apart—my insides taken out. And I was able to role-play this thing through and go on several trips that Jason took me on and I was really *involved* within those twenty-four hours. I was all there all the time, just about. I didn't sleep at all and I couldn't eat. I was very into everything. Everyone. I was turned on to guys and all my feelings were really coming to the surface. A lot of hatred and a whole lot of love and warmth and anger—all mixed in at the same time.

And when I went back to Frieda and we talked about it, and how it happened so successfully, I developed feelings about this man. He'd been just fabulous for me. I felt that I was like a flower that was beginning to open up. I had fanta-sies of going to his office, sitting down and talking to him. I became friendly with people I had met at his marathon. I thought they were really groovy and into a lot of stuff. I got into a lot of exciting things that summer, I felt, because of them. My husband is very conservative and his life is a kind of narrow thing. He didn't want to go to any concerts. He didn't want to try marijuana—which I had tried and hadn't felt very good about and so had cut that off. And all of a sudden I was turned on to lots of kinds of things, and I was still rebelling against the middle-class background I had come from. And all these guys were turned on to me and I said, like, "Hey! I'm a woman! And I'm attractive. And like men like me. And they like my body, and what's inside of me."

And I started to show it. I started to respond to men and to my feelings more freely.

I didn't see Jason after the marathon until this party, which I think was about three weeks to a month later. He was leaving for another city and I called to say that I wanted to do another marathon with him before he left. I was tight on money and my husband didn't want me to go, but that made no difference. I was going to another marathon anyway. Then he told me that his patients were giving him a going-away party as he was about to go off to the East coast for a year of work there.

I steered clear of him practically the whole night of the party. You know, I went up to him and I spoke to him a little bit. But I watched him. And every time I turned around his hands were down another woman's dress. Like I couldn't get over this. And they all loved it. I mean they all thought it was out of sight. I don't know how drunk he was or anything else, and I was steering clear. Then one guy came in whom I'd met at the marathon and I was sitting and rapping with him and I said, "You know it's really funny. I've really steered clear of Jason all night. I'm not sure why."

And he said, "Well, come on. Let's go over and sit next to him." So we did. Then Jason turned around to me and we started kissing, and he started to touch my breasts and he said, "Come on. Let's go inside." Finally I was in a bathroom with him and I'm shaking and he said, "Hey, I don't like this. Will you come back to my office with me?"

And I didn't know what I wanted to do. I was really involved in a battle. I finally said, "Okay. Screw it. I'm going to go. What's going to happen?"

It was like from that point on we both got involved in these fantasies. I had sex with him and it was great, like I've never experienced. It was like all of my dreams. It was free and beautiful and I was able to keep coming and I was amazed that, for a man of his age, he was really quite good. We took a bath together and a shower together and it was lovely. At one point he said to me, "Why don't you look at yourself in a mirror and see how beautiful you are? You should appreciate yourself." I guess we spent about two hours together. I felt drunk at the end of it. I felt high. I felt beautiful. I felt, "Gee. I really am a woman."

That was the thing that he made me feel most. That I really was a woman. And a lovely woman. My body was lovely. And it wasn't deformed, as I thought it was.

And I did tell (well, everyone was aware that we had left the party together). It was like out at that point. His patients knew. Like this guy knew, the one who brought me over to sit with Jason, and word got around. And I had become somewhat friendly with one of the women at the marathon. She was a few years older than I. And I did one day sit down and tell her about it, which I felt was a very foolish thing—I shouldn't have done that. I shouldn't have told anyone about it.

Then Jason sort of caught on to this, and started playing this girl against me. By then she and I were very close. This all happened a few days later. Then I sort of started to hear that this wasn't the first time he had done this with a patient of his.

He'd taken this patient and screwed her, and gotten involved with that patient and so on. I was getting this feedback from these other people who had been at the marathon with him. My feeling at that point was, "Gee. I'm not so special." Because I thought I was really special, you know, that he'd want to screw me, and that we'd have intercourse and get involved in this affair. And then all of a sudden, I began to feel not so special. And I began to feel like I had been used. And I was angry. I called him up and I told him. I told him I wasn't going to another marathon with him, and that I was very angry. And that he had put this girl, who I had been very close to, at odds with me. He had asked this girl and me to travel with him to a psychiatric convention to do a demonstration. And he was also going to give a marathon there the same weekend.

I said that I was very concerned and disturbed and upset, and he asked me to have dinner with him to talk about it. And I said, "Okay. I'll do that." And before I went I decided like, "Hey. He's not going to lay me tonight. That's all there's to it. I'm just going to set things straight and that's the end." And we had dinner and we got high, and we ended up going back to his apartment, and having sex. Again it was lovely and beautiful. But I decided I wouldn't go to another marathon of his.

He was afraid that I would expose him to his patients. He never said that directly. He just said, "I think it's a better idea—you're right—if you don't come." Because I felt I couldn't get anything out of him as a therapist anymore, that our relationship was too tied up. Also, if I went to the marathon he didn't want me to talk about this, and how could I not talk about it?

Then I said, "You know, the date of the marathon is my birthday. How would you like to give me a birthday present?"

And he said, "Sure, what's that?" And I said, "Would you still like me to do the demonstration?" And he said, "Yes." So he was going to take me with him for the weekend, that's what it was.

So the marathon was held and I didn't go. But I was torn —I did feel the fact that he now denied his relationship with me as a therapist, whereas I felt that he still was to a certain extent. And I felt that this marathon might be an opportunity for me to do something more.

I spent the weekend with him at the convention and had a marvelous time. The demonstration was great. He was doing some work on people taking trips without the use of drugs, without acid. So I was taking like an acid trip without acid.

And I went through a trip into my body and so on. It was very successful. And of course he was successful because I was so good.

And we had a great weekend. We played little sadistic games with each other. That's how I met Don. We went to a panel discussion that Jason was on on Sunday morning. And I saw Don. And I thought he was a pretty groovy young guy. We started to talk and—oh! Jason had Mary along (the other girl I mentioned) to do a demonstration also. And I was very uptight about him screwing her. She was a regular patient of his and like I didn't want that to happen. Like I wanted to have him exclusively to myself. He kept telling me like, "Don't worry. That's not going to happen." But the more he kept saying it, the more I wondered. I had fantasies that I'd go back to the hotel room and she'd be sprawling on the bed with him. And that was frightening. So when I saw Don, I had lunch with him and I disappeared, and Jason couldn't find me.

And when I came back he was furious. Like why hadn't I been there to have lunch with him? So I played a little game with him and I said, "You know, I thought you wanted to be with your colleagues and not hang around with me. And that's okay, so I split." Which was a lot of bullcrap, but I was saying, "I can play the game as well as you."

I didn't know that he was really going to screw Mary, but I had the feeling that this was the kind of a person he was. He'll take something and he'll play odds against it. That he's going to get the most he can out of this situation. So I left early and this girl Mary stayed on with him. And I was really panicky to get back because I felt he'd get to her—you know? She had said to me at one point that she wasn't interested in going to bed with him and da, da, da, and she went on and on with it. Yet when she saw me with him, all of a sudden that had changed. I was very uptight about that, and that our friendship really was just splitting apart.

So I came back home. And I saw him off to the East coast. And that was the last time I saw him—at that weekend and at the plane. So, in all, I spent that weekend with him and two other nights.

We wrote to each other for about two months, until my husband discovered the letters that Jason was sending to me. Which were straight out: like he loved the inside of me and the whole business—explicit details, how he loved it and it was great, how he missed me and so on. And that was that, and I stopped writing. And then I wrote to him about two months after that, to tell him why I had stopped writing and also wondered why he had stopped writing to me, because his last letter had not implied anything to the effect that he was going to stop writing. Then he wrote back a very curt typed letter, evidently written by a secretary, saying that he was very angry that I had run around telling people about our relationship, which I really hadn't done. I mean his patients knew about it. They knew about it before I told them.

What he had done that weekend at the convention, really, was to exploit the whole thing in front of all these people. He just opened by saying like, "Here's this chick and I'm having an affair with her. She's my patient." He didn't actually say to people he was having an affair with me, but he'd introduce me as Kathy. And the way he'd talk to me, people thought I was married to him.

The way he walked around with me and held on to me and the way he displayed himself toward me it was very evident that I just wasn't a patient of his.

People would say, "How do you know Jason?" And I would say, "I *was* his patient" (because I know you can get into a real hassle about that). I was at that time trying to protect him—from what I don't know—because he didn't try to protect himself. And then he hung that shit on me in that typed letter. He turned around to me and told me that I told everyone about it. That I was telling the world about it—

which I hadn't done. And that was the last time I heard from him. That was it.

Anyway, I had hidden all of Jason's letters. But I guess I hadn't hidden them well. I guess I did want my husband to find them. One night, after I had come home from the house of a girl friend, Alice, he said, "I sorted some papers," and I knew what it was.

I said, "So you found the letters," or something like that. And he said, "Yes. How could you have done such a disgusting thing?"

At first I denied it. Which was crazy. Because it was all there on paper. But I said that he was really just carrying it to an extreme and that it really wasn't so and da, da, da. And then I realized, "Fuck it. That's what happened." And I said, "Okay. It happened."

What could I do then? I couldn't tell him I was sorry, because I wasn't sorry for what had happened. Because I felt like it was an important experience for me. So I said, "Why didn't you call me at Alice's when you found the letters?"

He played up this whole scene. He said he went out in the snow and he walked by the river, which just makes me laugh because I think it's a little melodramatic. I mean, why didn't he call me at Alice's instead of waiting four hours? I thought that was just ridiculous. And he went over to some friends, Bobby and Amy—at which point I became very uptight. The story had now been spread around; now friends of mine were involved.

At first he denied to me that he had told them anything and I said, "You're a liar. I know you told them." And then he said, "Yes," he had told them.

And I said, "What did Bobby say?", and he said Bobby said he couldn't stay with his wife if she did something like that.

And then Amy said that if he really loved me, things could

be worked out; that maybe it was just as well that it had happened and that it came out.

But my husband at this point saw that there was no way out but a divorce. I was going to go along with him, I guess in part because I wanted it, and in part because I wasn't going to have to live the rest of my life saying, "I'm sorry," and kissing his ass.

So I said, "Listen. I'm not going to tell you not to, because I can't live this way." And then I said to him, "Is there anything that would make you change your mind about leaving?" Because I really felt that this was it, but I guess at that point I must have gotten frightened.

And he said, "Yes. You'll have to stop going to therapy and marathons. Group therapy and marathons. Because this is where your troubles come from. It would never have happened if you hadn't been to those marathons."

And I said, "I couldn't possibly do that, especially if I was going to go into divorce proceedings." I said I would need a group more than ever, probably, that I just wouldn't do it. And that we would have to get a divorce if that was the way out.

At this point we were sitting on the bed and talking and he had said that he had cried and I sort of wished that I could have seen him cry because I'd seen him angry and full of hate, but I've never seen anything like that. I was sort of amazed that he was able to cry. At which point he sort of reneged. He said he loved me and that there was nothing he could do about groups, he could see. He tried to make me swear that I would never go to another marathon and I said I wouldn't go to one for at least six months. That was as far as I could promise him. At this time I had just been to one of Frieda's, so I felt that I had had enough for a while. I had had two marathons within two months.

Before this, I had encouraged Richard to have sexual relations with other women. I didn't know how much real experience he himself had had. I knew only that he had had one other affair before we were married. He did tell me that night that there was a girl at his graduate school who wanted to have an affair with him and he had said, "No." What I felt he was saying to me was that he really had had the affair. Although at this point he was denying it, I called him a liar, but that was okay because I had said to him, "Like maybe if you got more sexual experience, things would be better for us in bed." Because they stank.

We're still together. I don't know if it will last. It's been five months now since he found out about Jason. And it's funny . . . at times, I've suspected him but I've thought, "Well, okay. Maybe it's good if that happens. Maybe things will be better for us." And he has turned back to me and said, "You were the one that went out and got fucked."

I've suggested to him that we go for counseling, but he won't go for any therapy at all.

Now I'm buying things pretty much as I want them, and with my work and his part-time job the money is there. There is still some hassle about money but I've opened my own savings account and I'm putting money away. I guess I'm putting money away because I know the inevitable will come. That I'm going to become so strong that I won't want him. It's a very parasitic kind of relationship. We live on each other's sadomasochism.

I torture him sexually. I want to bite him, I want to torture him, and verbally I really cut him. I bite him when we're making love and when I'm sucking him off. And he says it hurts. I get the feeling like I just want to claw him. Right now I'm involved in a whole thing about torture—and pain and pleasure. And he tortures me by being alive.

He's beaten me—not really beaten me but given me a good sock. I scream and yell at him now. I've gotten to that point, I tell him to get the fuck out of my life. And I'll pick up on things and really carry them to an extreme. I really drive him crazy until he starts throwing the food down on the floor and the plates go flying and the chairs go flying and then I'll stand there and I'll laugh at him. And I'll just laugh. I can laugh, laugh, laugh. It drives him crazy, that I could absolutely stand there. But I think it's so ludicrous that I just laugh.

As far as the effect of the affair with Jason is concerned, I think it's had a relatively, oh I don't know—I've analyzed the thing so many times I'm sick of it but—he did make me feel like a woman. He made me realize my womanhood. And my sexuality. And my sensuality. And that I should go with these feelings. It's interesting. Richard thinks I'm better in bed now than I ever was. Jason just sort of opened up a whole world to me in terms of sexual freedom. And I really have tried to stay with those feelings.

I felt real love for this man. Not love that I'd want to marry him, but love in that he had given me something very special. And for that I loved him. But I don't love him any more. I really don't.

I sat down last night to analyze why I was coming here to talk to you today. And I guess I do want some revenge on Jason as a doctor.

I would like to destroy all doctors. Because I feel they have been very destructive to me.

Like I hate doctors and I have rage for them, and I'm frightened of them. And when I first got engaged to Richard he intended to become one although he couldn't get into a medical school. But I guess it's a symbolic sort of destruction. I'd like to destroy Jason and my husband, and say like, "You fucking doctors! You're not that goddamned powerful." So even if Jason gave me something, he's still a doctor and I still feel that what he did was unethical. Because I was his patient, and he was no longer able to give me treatment, I felt, after I had had this sexual relationship with him.

So I've had four therapists now (including Jason). My current group is with someone new. In comparing them I feel that as a result of the positive experience at the marathon with Jason—as a therapist—I did go back to Frieda and I had an extremely positive marathon with her. And I had a lot of good stuff that I was able to get into—explore—because of Jason. I can't separate my involvement from my therapy with him. He had a great impact on my life and I'd have to rate him Number One—maybe Number Two—among the therapists I've seen. He did have a great impact on my life.

But I think as a lover he had more impact on me than as a therapist—and the two together were sort of dynamite. Because, as I have been able to evaluate since the marathon, he's good as a therapist. But he's only good up to a point. I think everyone has their limitations in what they're able to give and what they come to with the situation. I think that, strictly as a therapist alone, he's more limited than other therapists that I've been with.

I was attracted to Jason then not for his body but because he was a great man. Like he was this great man who was beautiful, and he wanted me. How groovy. But within the situation I realized my own power as a person—as for example with Don, the guy I met at the convention. And I realized that Jason didn't like the idea that I had spent time with another man while I was with him. Like that came through very clearly.

My husband never learned about my affairs after Jason. He told me that if I ever did have another one he would leave me. I guess that one day I could say to him, "Well, I've had another one. It's time for you to go."

Recently I've stopped screwing around. Like I'm not seeing a guy that I was seeing this summer. And I'm not seeing Jason. I'm not seeing my friend's husband anymore. I'm not seeing anyone really except for Tom. Just like on a once-a-month shot. I'm spending more time alone. I don't mind it.

I have tried to reach Richard on an emotional level. To

tell him about my feelings now, and as a child. He knows that the marriage, as far as I'm concerned, stinks in many ways. For him it's not going anywhere either. He says I'm not making the marriage. He's putting it all on me, which is a lot of bullshit. I refuse to accept total responsibility for this marriage not working out. Because I don't think it's all my fault.

I don't think I'll see Jason again when he gets back. I have no desire to see him anymore. It's the end. He did come in from the East once, I know, and I sort of wondered once about seeing him and stuff, but it's past and it's gone. And it was, and it will never be anymore. And it never could be the same again. And that's the reality of the situation.

AUTHOR'S POSTSCRIPT

Kathy seems to be a young woman in the unenviable position of trying to regain her womanliness from the men (doctors) whom she feels deprived her of it. And it is hard to feel feminine when filled with the resentments that she harbors.

Longing and revenge are everywhere.

What evidence there is suggests to me that it is she (and not Jason or her friends or other doctors) who plays people against one another, and that it is she who is really quite cold and callous. That is not to say that the same qualities may not exist in those with whom she surrounds herself.

It is hard to believe that Jason was so concerned about what people thought about their relationship as she would like to believe. For apparently his passions were well known to his patients. And he certainly did nothing to hide his lustiness at his party or at the psychiatric convention.

Kathy's later concern with ethics seems to arise only after she discovers that she is not the only woman patient that Jason has been involved with. Thus his affirmation of her desirableness is not quite as rewarding as she would have it be. The scales then tip to the vengeful side.

Kathy describes Jason as a very lusty man with indiscriminate sexual appetites—someone who might have done what he did regardless of the consequences. However, I don't think we can make such a judgment unless all his female patients were to be interviewed. For it is equally possible that Kathy's viewpoint is clouded by resentment against nonexclusiveness.

Certainly Jason's reactions to her seem straightforward and honest. While I have no doubt that he was intimate with Kathy—and more or less indiscriminately with numerous other patients—in order to satisfy his own desires, he nonetheless satisfied some of her needs.

Her statement that Jason did much to affirm her as a woman ("he made me realize my womanhood") seems unquestionable. I doubt that anyone could have done more in this regard, given the horns of the dilemma on which she was caught.

6

JESSIE

"We were friends and lovers"

She is a Ph.D. candidate in clinical psychology, age twenty-six, of medium height and build, with long, straight sandy hair. She wears no make-up. She is pretty, although not in any extraordinary way.

She relates her experiences in a matter of fact, cut-and-dried way, all the while being attentive to serving me coffee and tea (the interview is held in her home in California). She is very much the good hostess.

She exudes the poise of a professional person.

I got out of college when I was twenty-one. I was very neurotic. It was my first year of teaching in an elementary school. And I started therapy.

I had a lot of difficulties in college as far as my relationship to myself was concerned. I was very unhappy, and I couldn't get help. Psychology wasn't as prominent, it wasn't as frequented, when I was in college, as it is now, and I thought I was normal. And I would cry. I just didn't want to be me. I went through such shit. But I didn't know that I was really neurotic. I just thought that was the way it was. I was just very depressed and unhappy and found it very difficult to be with myself. Very painful.

I was able to function. I graduated from college in three and a half years and made dean's list, I did well. I participated in extracurricular activities, I dated. I didn't have particularly successful relationships—I got involved with one guy who was engaged and we had a lovely relationship until it was time for him to get married—that kind of thing. And I had friends.

Still, I was extremely critical of myself, uncomfortable with myself. It was the obsessional kind of thing: I'd go over "What did I say, what did I do, what did I do wrong?" and hate myself intensely. For stupid things like doing something at a fraternity party. I felt very inadequate and very rejectable and I was so anxious then that I used to feel that there were tons on my shoulders.

I never knew why. I took some psych courses but I just never really related them to myself. And I would always pick very difficult kinds of men—men who were very hard to get. And if you got one, boy, well—it was impossible. Like this guy with the engagement who really liked me, whom I really liked. When we started the relationship he was getting married in a month. We had been friends for a long time and then physical stuff came into it.

I had had intercourse for the first time when I was a senior in high school—sixteen. I had gone with the guy from freshman to senior in high school and I had felt very guilty. A nice Jewish girl, you know? Very guilty. Couldn't tell anyone. So I had lots of guilt feelings with sex. In college (until my senior year) I didn't have any sexual relations, petting, perhaps, but nothing deeper. I wanted to, because I had a sex drive, but I couldn't let myself because I would've annihilated myself for doing that. When I think about it, anytime I even petted with a guy or got at all physically involved I felt so guilty about it because I had loved the first guy—or felt that I loved him. And I felt you had to be in love and so I just couldn't do it.

When I started teaching—I really enjoyed teaching—I got involved with a guy and it wasn't successful. He was another one of these difficult kind of guys. My sister was in therapy and she kept pushing me to go to the clinic on the campus. So finally I went.

At the interview I was most afraid that the guy was going to say to me, "There's nothing wrong with you, girlie," you know, "grow up!" Something like that. Which would've meant to me I had to go on like this forever and ever and ever. And at that point I was driving to work crying, because I was just falling apart. I was having such problems with depression.

When I graduated college I wanted to be a singer. I had done a lot of singing in college. So I decided to give myself six free months to see what this field was like before I did something like a "right" thing, like teaching.

I got a vocal coach and I started to go to auditions and things like that and of course it was difficult. I hadn't had the training and I didn't have the diction. And I'd be at home. I was living with my parents and their friends would say, "Well what are you doing now?" And I would say, like, "Nothing," and I felt mortified. I felt like nothing because I was doing nothing. It was a very difficult thing for me to cope with, so I had to get out of the singing thing. I couldn't cope with the lack of structure. So I went into therapy.

And this was with a guy who was in training. I think he was getting a master's degree. I don't even know if he was going for his doctorate. He was a minister. And he wasn't my type of guy. He wasn't the kind of guy I'd be attracted to. Kind of average looking.

The whole thing was a supportive relationship. It was a helpful relationship. After I had gone to see him his words were, "Yes, I think I can help you." Which meant to me, like, "Wow, maybe there's some hope." That relationship continued for six months—the therapeutic one. And I had no sexual feelings toward him at all.

At times I felt that he had such feelings toward me. He'd

say something like, "I'm not the kind of guy you would go for," and I would feel like, "Wow! I really don't want to hurt his feelings." Yet I couldn't be that honest in the relationship. I just wasn't ready to be. And so I don't know how I responded to that (it was six years ago) but I'm sure I didn't say, "No." Then he went to a town two hundred miles up the coast, where he was doing more work. And a couple of times in a panic I would drive for four hours and have a session with him up there.

One time when I was up there he said to me, "Look, I want to deal with my own feelings. And I feel that I'm sexually attracted to you and I feel that by telling you this it will help me to deal with it. How do you feel about that?"

And I couldn't handle it at all. I smiled and I said, "Well, that's very nice." I didn't feel it was very nice at all. I felt very upset by it. But I couldn't be honest with him. I couldn't tell him.

I felt very anxious, like, "Now what am I supposed to do?" I was very concerned with doing the right thing, pleasing him, being—you know, I didn't want him not to like me.

If he would have made any kind of demands on me— which he didn't do at all—I don't know what I would have done. It would have been very difficult for me to say "No." This was someone I needed, I didn't want to offend him, I wouldn't want to be rude. Luckily he didn't. If he had, I don't know that I would've slept with him because I wasn't attracted to him physically. But if he had put his arms around me or kissed me or something, I probably would have submitted and been really torn. So that was that thing. And then I stopped going up there and I don't know how much later I got into therapy with Bill.

I wasn't in therapy for about a year, I guess. And I was still pretty unhappy. And a friend of mine told me about Bill. He was a clinical psychologist and he was taking a psychology course with him and recommended that I see him. And that's what I did. I was in private therapy with him for about six months and a group for about six months. So I was with him for about a year.

That therapeutic relationship was very important to me. Because the emphasis was on thinking, and I owned every irrational thought in the book. So it was very helpful in lots of ways.

I wanted Bill's approval and I wanted very much to be a good patient, which is my style. I realized at a group workshop this past November that the way I get approval is by being seductive. So I'm sure that I was very seductive to Bill in the relationship. Because I wanted him to like me. He was warm. He was a little flirty but not seriously so, which would have been threatening to me.

I would say one of the major themes in the therapeutic relationship was that I wanted his approval. I wanted to be a good patient. So I would report back, "I'm thinking clearly and I'm blah, blah, blah," and inside it was conflicting emotions, craziness, anger, all kinds of things happening. But I knew the way I was "supposed" to be thinking.

I couldn't talk about the irrational stuff or even of my having to be a good patient. I wouldn't tell. And I was a "good patient." I kept all my neurosis, although I did learn to think more rationally. But it didn't recondition my emotional stuff at all. What I did learn were things like, it's not so terrible to make a mistake—you don't have to be perfect. I learned to tell myself these things. I learned to be able to listen to what I was telling myself. I learned to be able to tune in on a lot of the very surface level shit that I would drive myself crazy with—like things have to go a certain way or a catastrophe will occur. And that was very helpful. And I was more able to cope with my depression. I was able to talk myself out of it. My self-esteem was a little better, but the depression wasn't removed. The rational exercise prepared me to go into deeper therapy. And it helped me in functioning in my life. Like in terms of having more energy. You have more energy when you can cut down on some of the bullshit.

It got me going for my doctorate. Bill influenced me tremendously in ways like that. I did a lot of very concrete things. I could get myself out of shitty things if I really tuned into it. I was more in control. But it was all on a surface level. All the undercurrents of conflicts and deep, deep feelings about myself just weren't affected. But my ego controls were being strengthened and I was able to function much more efficiently.

Not, though, in male-female relationships. A month after I got into therapy with Bill I started a relationship with Curt, a married guy, and kept the relationship all through my therapy. I just broke it off a while ago. I don't know how much better I am now in that area. I imagine I'm somewhat better, but I don't know if it's significantly so or not.

After therapy with Bill I thought I was finished with therapy. Because I could say everything right. In group, I was the group leader. It was terrific. It was great for me as far as ego and all that stuff was concerned. I was feeling good. I wasn't getting any more help because I knew how to think. I wouldn't tell them what was happening, underneath, because they would just tell me I was thinking wrong. Well, I *knew* that I wasn't really believing the right things. So I'd go in that merry-go-round and that was like for shit. So there was nothing else there.

I think what's important here is that I could never really be honest with Bill, either. I could never tell him that there were feelings of irrationality underneath, that I was driving myself nuts, and that I knew how to think right and it wasn't helping. I couldn't do that because I couldn't chance his disapproval. I was seeing him as a man, who was my therapist, whom I really wanted to like me.

I don't remember specifically but I always wore something

cute when I went to see Bill, and fixed my hair and it was a bright spot in my week and that kind of thing. There were so many secondary kinds of things involved that it really impeded my being honest. I later realized I had to go into therapy with a woman.

A year after I got out of therapy with Bill I decided that I had to get back into therapy because I was as crazy as ever. Friends told me to go to this psychiatrist who was a European and a Freudian. I would lie down on the couch. It was very different from any other stuff I had ever experienced, but I thought, "I'll try anything. Let me see what it's like."

He wasn't approving at all, this new therapist, and all my projections really started coming out. He would just sit there. I was sure, in the two months I went to him, that he didn't know my name. I was positive that he was watching the clock all the time. There was no positive stuff. There was no smile, there was no—I couldn't get him to approve of me. I couldn't manipulate. I wasn't aware of trying to manipulate him. I just hated him. I hated him. And he would say to me, "Tell me how you feel about me," and I'd say, "Well, I think you're a very nice man," or something like that.

I couldn't be honest with him either. I couldn't be honest with anyone. I couldn't tell him how I felt, really, because he wouldn't like it. But nothing worked. I couldn't get to this guy on any level. So I got out of therapy with him.

In therapy with a woman I was able to be honest. I had no difficulties in saying how I'd feel. And I've been with this woman Gestalt psychiatrist, Eleanor, now for almost two years. And for the first time I was able to say, "Fuck off! This is how I feel." All of a sudden I began to be in touch with what was happening inside of me. I didn't have to please Eleanor. I accepted the fact that she had taken me as a patient and liked me, and I didn't have to seduce her.

Obviously the problems in my life are with men. I feel, really, that the therapy with Bill was playing into my own manipulations. It was defeating my purpose, which was getting better. And by being able to seduce him, (even though I didn't seduce him when I was in therapy, literally, there was a slight flirtation going on that affected the relationship) we didn't get into what was happening.

This seduction thing never came up when he was my therapist. Later on I became a student where he was teaching. As a matter of fact, while I was in therapy I was getting my master's at one place and I switched to get it where he was because the program was better there. But he didn't even know that I was in psychology or getting my master's in psychology until one day I was discussing how dissatisfied I was where I was because the people there offered a terrible program and I told him that I was switching.

This was after I stopped seeing him in treatment. When I started at his school he became my advisor. I took some courses with him and soon after that I became his course assistant, too. I graded his papers and got paid by the university.

Being in school placed our relationship on a whole different basis. We flirted and I wanted to go out with him. And I knew if I went out with him that we'd go to bed, because I felt that that was his style; that if I wanted to go out with him, that that would be part of it. So if I really didn't want to go to bed with him I wouldn't have gone out with him.

Eventually he asked me out. I had broken off with my boy friend Curt for a while, and when Bill learned this he asked me for a date. And we went out and returned to my apartment and went to bed.

Bill was divorced, in his late thirties, an attractive man, although not really my type physically. In the beginning I was very up-tight because I wanted to do the right thing, but I never felt those feelings of—is he going to call again? Will I see him tomorrow?—because we had an understanding. Like our relationship would be one where we would see each other, but I never expected to see him like six nights a week or every weekend or anything like that. I didn't have crazy expectations and so it was very nice. Plus the fact that I wasn't in love with him or anything like that, so I didn't want too much from him.

He would send me little notes and he'd do sweet things, which was nice. And our relationship didn't go on that long because I went back with my boyfriend.

Then I broke up with my boy friend again and went out with Bill a few times and then went to South America for a month.

Bill wrote me lovely letters. And my boy friend wrote me too: love letters saying that he was leaving his wife and that he couldn't live without me. And I was really in conflict because I really loved Curt and I wondered what I was going to tell Bill. That Curt was leaving his wife for me? I believed it, right?

And when I came back, I was in conflict and I started seeing Curt again. But there was never really any problem with Bill because Bill was never madly in love with me. I mean he liked me and it was nice. We would go out once in a while.

Bill and I never had a romantic relationship. We were friends/lovers/friends. Maybe for a week or so it was romantic but—first of all came his schedule. There was a time factor. I never had illusions of being in love with him. I wasn't like neurotically crazy about him like I had been about this guy Curt I had been seeing for so many years. It was exciting. It was challenging having something with Bill. And it worked out nicely because we're still very good friends.

In the beginning Bill would talk about himself, about what he would be doing. I was interested in that and I'd encourage that. I wouldn't talk about me. I wouldn't talk about what I was doing or anything like that. Or very little. Or things that related to him. I would pull from him. He responded to being listened to, to being approved of. And at times he'd say to me, "Well, what do you think about, or what do you think I'm doing here, or where's my craziness?" Well, my feeling was—how do you expect me to tell you? I felt this guy knows it all. Me? I'm learning from him.

And I would also learn a great deal. I would get a lot of information and stuff like that about psychology and stuff that I was interested in. It was not, however, a relationship in which I was being me. I was being a part of me but it was a very isolated part. It was a part that I would think that Bill would like. That was in the beginning when we were first lovers. It was easier for me to maintain it because he wasn't asking anything of me. I didn't have to be myself. I didn't have to talk about myself. I could listen to him. So it worked out very nice.

Then we split. I went back with my boy friend. I didn't see Bill for a while. And later on, when he and I went to Baja California, we were already friends and lovers, more than the romantic kind of thing.

We spent about three or four days together in Baja. And at times I was intensely annoyed with him. And at times I was obnoxious and annoying, which I never had been before with him. I returned home earlier than he did and there were very warm feelings between us when we left. Not the kind of feelings that we were really compatible enough to get into a serious one-to-one relationship. But it was much realer, because at that time I needed his approval less. I could *be* more. And anyway, over a three-day period of time you can't be so sweet and nice all the time, especially when you're a bitch inside.

But, you know, even at that time if I didn't want to sleep with him, if I didn't want to have intercourse, I couldn't tell him. Because I would be afraid of hurting his ego or something like that. So I would wind up doing it—not that it was terrible; it was good.

But I isolated the physical aspect of our relationship. It was not a major part. Sometimes I would have orgasms and sometimes not. Sex was relatively insignificant in terms of our relationship and I wouldn't take very much from it. And I didn't give very much to it. It was pleasant at first and maybe not so pleasant when I began to feel that maybe I didn't want to sleep with him and that maybe I would have to tell him.

Eventually we just stopped going out. He knew I was back with Curt—we'd talk about Curt. It wasn't messy in any way, and we never saw each other that much.

For Bill, I think it was a pleasant relationship, a pleasant encounter with a lot of warmth. What continued from it was a friendship. I think it was meaningful in a friends' sense. I don't think it had a special meaning as a lover kind of relationship, but as friends, as caring. And I've got a lot of appreciation for him in lots of ways. He's helped me a good deal in lots of practical ways. Like he went out of his way to get me into the doctoral program. I feel that Bill would help me in any way if he could, if I needed something from him. And I would reciprocate. I have very good feelings for him.

I think his own head isn't straight in a lot of ways. I learned that after I became his friend—not as his patient. That he's cut off from lots of his feelings, that he avoids a great deal, but I don't really want to go into that. Allowing myself to see it enabled me to deal with it. It didn't change my feelings about Bill at all. It didn't change what I learned from him or what I feel about him.

I feel that my therapeutic relationship with Bill would have been a hell of a lot more profitable for me if he would've tuned into what I was doing. I was seducing him. Which was being cute, which was being all these things to get him to like me. So I couldn't be honest with him. Just as I couldn't be when I was fucking with him, I couldn't be in the relationship with him because I was trying to gain. It's the same thing. I don't know why he didn't notice it, but we didn't deal with it at all. So I was accomplishing my neurotic goal when my problem was having an honest relationship with a man. Even in a therapeutic relationship I wasn't able to be honest.

And that is why I don't think that it's beneficial, basically, for a male therapist to fuck his women patients. Because it's a common thing that women seek approval by this kind of manipulation. And they're afraid to be what they are as human beings. They're afraid to show what they're feeling, what they're really thinking, because they're needy or dependent or whatever. But if they can be good sexually, or if they can get a man—the therapist—to like them physically, well, that's acceptance. And what do you try to do with daddy when you're a little girl? You want to get him to fuck you or to love you, whatever it may be. Not necessarily to take you to bed, but you want him sexually in some way. I know I did. Like I wanted Father to come in and kiss me goodnight, or whatever. And it's the same thing. If it's not worked through and it's just fed, I don't see that as being helpful to the patient.

I don't feel that my going to bed with Bill was detrimental in any way. Had it been during the treatment it would've been much worse because in treatment with me he was more of a figure. By the time I went to bed with him he was already fairly human. I saw him in school. Some students liked him, some students didn't. But as his patient I was more or less idolizing him, and I would have been so tense, I would have been so petrified, that I would have done something wrong or fucked it up. And if he rejected me after he fucked me and he was my therapist, I don't know if I could have handled that at all. Which is another thing.

Bill was *very* important in my life. Although he didn't help me much emotionally as Eleanor has, as far as my life and functioning is concerned, no one has influenced me more than he. I wouldn't be doing what I'm doing professionally, if he hadn't pushed me and showed a lot of confidence in me. And I would have to say that his influence as friend and lover was equal to that of his being my therapist.

In summary, my experience with Bill was a positive one, I'd say. This is terrible, because I don't really approve of the whole thing—therapists having sex with patients—but if I had to rate it on a scale where ten is tops, from where I was and everything like that, I would give it an eight. It's terrible because intellectually I wouldn't think of ranking it so high, but when I get in touch with my feelings that's what comes out.

AUTHOR'S POSTSCRIPT

Once again the therapist (whatever his limitations in perceptiveness might have been) has related without apparent deception to his former patient.

Jessie comes across very much as an intellectual, somewhat obsessive in her thinking, as opposed to being physically in touch with herself. It would be hard for me to imagine her having an intensely physical relationship with anyone. I would tend to attribute some part of her sensual indifference to Bill to this quality in her.

Given the orientation of Bill's therapy, with its emphasis on rational thinking, I don't see how he could have been more effective as a therapist than he was. Indeed, Jessie's need to please men was not taught to her by any therapist. She told me that she caught herself at it inadvertently later on.

What was most striking to both of us was the gap between her theoretical speculations about intimacy between therapists and patients and the actuality of her own experience.

The relationship with Bill comes across as a reasonable and mature one between two thinking people.

7

MARCUS

"It was like a Grand Guignol"

A thirty-two year old writer, he is a handsome, slightly built man with intense eyes, a slight facial twitch, and a full head of curly, black hair. He looks like photographs of the young Karl Marx.

His voice is deep, sure, and compassionate.

I was twenty three. I had just come back from overseas. I was in the army and I had been married for about eleven months to an Asian girl. And that had just fallen apart. I had walked out because I couldn't stand the pressure of it. And I was at a school in California taking a course in the psychology of personality with Susan. She was just kind of a warm, friendly woman. Her whole class consisted of trying to find out what the experience was behind some theory she was teaching. So that instead of reading and giving tests so much, she would have us write papers about things that happened in our lives. I had never been exposed to anything like that before.

The first therapeutic thing I ever did in my life was to write a paper for her on *Why I Feel Inadequate*. She asked us to pick our own topic and I wrote a six-page paper for her in which I just spilled my heart out . . . for the first time in that way. And she gave me the paper back with an *A*-plus and she wrote at the bottom, "It sounds like from where you are now, you need therapy."

So I went to see her one day after class and—as she put it later—it seemed like I was "being held together by bailing wire and spit." I was living with two crazy Communists and my life was falling apart in front of my eyes. I was having massive depressions, anxieties where I would do nothing but like walk the streets for forty-eight hours. So when I went to talk to her, I said, "I'd love to get into therapy, but I don't know who, how, where, or anything like that." She said she was a certified psychologist and had a small experimental group which met after class, and she was experimenting on some psychophysical techniques.

So I went to one of her groups after class and we did very light breathing exercises, which I just found kind of relaxing and pleasant. And then she said, "I have an advanced group which meets in one of the student's houses. Would you like to come to that?" I pleaded having no money and she said it was free because it was still part of her private research.

So I went to this student's house and there were like twelve of us. We lay down on the living-room floor touching shoulder to shoulder. And we began a series of very deep breathing exercises, during the course of which I hyperventilated (I didn't know that at the time, but that's what was happening), so that my hands bunched up into fists and my face flushed and my ears tingled and my mouth got paralyzed. And I got very deep into a catatoniclike convulsion. Of course I immediately became the center of attraction for the entire group.

Everybody got up as Susan said, "Let's all gather around and watch what Marcus is doing," and I went through what I later found out was like acid flashes. Like for the first time in my life I felt my body.

I came up and I looked at my hand and it was the first time that I knew I had a hand. You know that first kind of experiential sense of being alive? Well, great waves of emotion ran through me. I had memories of childhood. I went through the whole shtick. I just started reliving everything, and then began crying. The weeping of relief—just getting in touch with all these things. Then I just kind of sat with it for about five minutes and began talking about myself.

And then, for the first time in my life, I heard my voice. In contrast to what I had just been feeling, I heard how flat and empty I sounded while rapping about who and what I was and what have you.

The session ended and Susan spoke to me afterward and said, "I think that I'd better see you privately also; in addition to the group." I didn't have any money, so she said she would take me for fifty cents a session. She said she wanted to have to charge me something and if that was all that I could afford, that was what she would take.

Now at this time she was coming out of a Rogerian* bag, she was deep into psychophysical techniques and she was stumbling on to Reich's** work, but she had never really read him. So like both of us were absolutely naive and blind as to what was happening. And we immediately began getting into these sessions whereby I would go in and take off my shoes, loosen all my clothing and lie down on the floor, and she would sit next to me and have me go into one of these deep-breathing things. And whenever I got tense, she would either suggest something, or have me go through a fantasy, or she would touch different parts of my body. And like, where I was at the time, this was all so overwhelming, that I had no sense of her as a person. She was just like a force which was moving me.

* Carl Rogers is a psychologist whose therapeutic approach is verbal and nondirective.
** Wilhelm Reich was a psychiatrist who pioneered a therapeutic approach based on loosening up the tensions in the patients' musculature—through deep breathing, touching, and excercising—as a way of freeing the mind of neurotic worries.

And she was like stumbling on to things that were more than she knew about. So she was very scared, too. So one of the things that was going on was like two children, kind of discovering something. We were *playing* therapist-patient, in a sense.

Physically she was a very big woman. Very tall and very fat. But a very beautiful face. And she was in her late forties at the time—married, with three children. She was living with her husband but having a very bad time of it and fucking a lot of people. She was having a lot of affairs at that time. I knew she was married and had children, but as far as the rest of it was concerned, she represented purity itself.

That phase of the therapy went on for a year. Simultaneously I did a group with her and another woman, who was a dancer. And they did animal exercises—the whole thing that Esalen* does now—only this was before there was an Esalen. And nobody knew what we were doing. All we knew was that if we lay down and relaxed and breathed, strange fantastic things would happen. So every week we met and got into some incredibly baroque relationships, where we wound up grabbing each other's cunts and cocks and, you know, hugging and kissing and doing all these things. *But none of it was sexy,* if you know what I mean. Because it was all under the rubric of therapy: We were making sure we got our therapeutic pound of flesh for what we went through. Meanwhile, I started to get involved in Susan's life.

At that point, therapy seemed to me to go like this: I was going through all of these changes that I knew nothing about and she was going through them with me. But in the back of her mind, she understood everything. She knew who I was and what I was going through and she was charting the course of the progress. And any time she could step in and say, "This

* Esalen is the well-known "growth center" at Big Sur, California, where new psychological techniques are being developed and tried—such as having participants decide what animal they are most like and then asking them to play-act at being that animal.

is what's going on." And of course that wasn't true. But that was my fantasy at the time.

A lot happened that year, like I woke up to colors for the first time and to what my body was about and to other people's faces and things like that. There was no immediate change in my initial complaints. I got to depend very heavily on the two times a week I saw her. It was like, if I could hold myself together until group or until I saw her, it was cool, because I knew I could get there and let myself fall apart. Which she encouraged. The crazier I went, the better she felt it was.

Meanwhile, she and this other woman were starting an institute of psychophysical techniques and awareness and all that. And I, because I started getting interested in psychology, started getting involved with it. So I started getting to know Susan socially, too. And I began to discover things like: she would have men and stay at the office overnight and she and her husband would fight all the time. He would call her and she would put him down very viciously. And this alternate picture began to grow in my mind of her, *which I absolutely refused to recognize*. The fact that she was fucking and didn't get along with her husband.

And then I met her children. And the children were all more neurotic than I was. I couldn't assimilate it, because she had to be perfect for me. She had to be the one who knew all. Otherwise I was in much deeper trouble than I thought I was. She was the only mainstay I had.

Simultaneously, of course, I started having affairs on and off with people in the group. Like one of the chicks was married and she and I were making it without her husband knowing, that kind of thing. Which was kind of dumb, but we would build up all of this sexual tension, which we couldn't feel as such in the group and then afterward we would go to my place for something and fuck. Yet we'd make no connection between fucking and what we were doing in the group.

The group was like church. It was like a different life. It had nothing to do with what went on during the day.

Of course, as I began meeting people who had their own problems I would send them to Susan: "You've got troubles? You're neurotic? Go see her." She began to be like a den mother. My entire social life began to revolve about her scene.

Then it reached a point in the therapeutic process where I could no longer take anything from her. She began to feel disgusting to me. And I had no way to tell her. Because all I could do was to tell her about what I was feeling that didn't have to do with her. So I would tell her about all my feelings with other women, right, and would never say, "I feel like I want to puke when you touch me." I wasn't allowed to tell the therapist that. So then the tension just got harder and harder. And it reached the point where I would go into therapy wanting to kill her. And one day it actually came.

We went into the room. She wanted me to lie down and I said, "No. I don't want to lie down." And we sat down on the couch, almost touching. I began to get into a heavy, heavy rap about myself and my body got extremely heavy. She said, "Do you want to lie down?" And I said "Yeah, but I don't want to lie down by myself." And she said, "You can lie on me." And she like reached over and brought me forward and put her arms around me and put my head on her belly. At first, it just felt like my mother. I just began weeping and sobbing and holding on to her and burrowing my head into her belly.

Then that spasm passed and I suddenly felt for the first time that I was lying on a couch with my arms around a woman's waist, with my face next to her cunt. And it suddenly got very sexy. I began kind of mindlessly groping up, working my way up her body until I was at her breast which was still behind a brassiere and a dress. And the only feedback I got from her was passive acceptance; that she would let me do what I

wanted, but that she wasn't feeling anything. That cut off the
sex feelings in me, and I got furiously angry.

I jumped up and I picked up a chair and I started smashing
the chair against the wall and she said, "What do you really
want to smash?" And I said, "I want to smash you!" And she
said, "Can you let yourself smash me?" I looked at her and
she was sitting there. She was filled with warmth and love and
concern. She also had the wickedest gleam of a cock-teaser in
her eyes. It just infuriated me and I just wanted to kill her, but
I couldn't because she was like mother and therapist.

I went into a rage, smashing things and pounding and hit-
ting on the floor until I let it all out. Then she came over and
comforted me. And I kicked her away and I said, "You give
me poison. There's nothing but poison that comes out of
you," and I pushed her away and I left the session.

Then I didn't come back for about two weeks. And when I
came back we started talking about what had happened. She
was sitting across the room from me, about fifteen feet away
and I was sitting in a straight-backed chair, looking down and
rapping about how I felt. And she said, "Why don't you look
at me?" I looked up and she was just beaming at me with love
and acceptance and warmth.

But it didn't feel like a therapist at that moment. It felt just
like a woman. And I looked at her and I said, "Susan, you're
beautiful" (as one would say to a woman), and she got up off
the chair and she walked across the room toward me. And she
put her arms around my neck and she said, "Thank God. I
thought you'd never notice," and began kissing me. And it's
very funny. I felt distinctly the obligation to go through a
sexual scene with her. It was like I wasn't really sexually
turned on, but it had reached the point where sex had arisen,
and she was now coming on to me and I had to respond.

She must have felt my tension because she pulled back and
she said, "Why don't we wait until my patients are finished
and then I'll come over to your place." So I went home and in

about an hour and a half she came. I was very nervous. I was polishing the book shelves and I was doing all kinds of things around the house. She came in and it was like I didn't know what to do with her. She kind of gathered me up and brought me to the bed.

We lay there for a while. And all of a sudden everything disappeared, all the images and fantasies, and she was just a woman. And she seemed totally in love with me and totally willing to do whatever I wanted. And so I began to be very rough, kind of testing her. Ripping off her clothes and grabbing her hair and pulling her hair very hard and biting her and things like that. And the more I did it, the more she dug it. And so I just let it all hang out and just fucked her very hard and very brutally and used her totally without any concern.

And then I came.

Afterwards she was all cuddly and warm and curled up in my arms and she felt like a six-year-old child. And then that scene began.

She went home that night and I called her during the week and said, "Should I come for my session?" "Oh no no," she said. "I don't think we can do therapy that way any more." She said, "That part of it is over. Why don't we just keep seeing each other." So we saw each other for about three months during which it was just like any other love affair.

I had been seeing her for a year before this happened. I was very excited by the sex, because I'd never been to bed with an older woman before. She was very fat, but very wet and juicy and just very rich. And she knew a lot, she knew how to lick and how to bite and how to suck and how to move her ass and all of that. And I'd never had a woman who was so experienced before. But at the same time I was going through all the changes of backing away from it. Like I was asking her for cues again, because I didn't know. I was just a kid.

And she said let's just keep doing the sex scene, in effect. I felt cheated that the therapy might end because from all the books I was reading in school at the time and what I was picking up from other people, therapy was supposed to help me come to terms with who I was. And it was getting more like I was getting into a scene with my therapist which was just as funny as all the other scenes I was in. It was very groovy and it was very exciting, but it didn't seem like it was going to be therapy anymore.

At the same time I had the feeling like she knew what she was doing, because she was the therapist. I had immense faith in her. Almost like a Catholic with the Pope. Like if she says we should fuck, maybe it's better for me. And the fantasy machine in the back of my head was saying, "Maybe I'll work all these things out with her," which would be like real therapy.

So I went back and for three months we went through this scene of fucking. And she wanted to be very romantic. She wanted a love affair. I learned only later on that she had love affairs with her patients all the time. She was looking for what she didn't get from her husband, her own neurotic needs and all that shit. But I didn't know that then. All I knew was that she started buying me things. Like buying me sweaters and wanting me to go dancing with her. And I was getting embarrassed. Because to go dancing with a fifty-year-old woman—I felt funny. The puritanical part of me wouldn't dig it.

And then she began nagging. Just like any woman. I didn't know what to do with it. Here was a woman who was the wisest woman in the world, nagging me because I wasn't paying enough attention to her, sounding for all the world like the other neurotic chicks that I knew. I began getting very uptight, and there was nobody I could talk to about it. The only one I could talk to was the one who was causing the problem.

It got to the point where I would go home and there would be knots in my belly and I didn't have the faintest notion—I didn't even have enough awareness to know that I was in a bag. All I knew was that I was unhappy and confused. I had slipped like right back into where I was a year before. Any gains that had been made in terms of insight were totally knocked on their ass.

One night I met her and she wanted to go to my place and I didn't want to. I was just very agitated. And so we took a walk. We walked about twenty blocks, and when we got to a corner I remember standing there, and I suddenly turned to her, and it all boiled up in me at once. I just started shouting all of these things at her: "You're a fat, sick old lady, you're neurotic. You're sick. You can't get along with your husband. Your kids are sick. Everything about you is sick. You're rotten. You make me sick." I just laid all that shit on her, and she just like collapsed.

She started crying and throwing her arms around my neck, and begging me not to leave her, going through this incredibly terrible scene. And the more she went into it, the more fierce I became.

All of a sudden I snapped into this role. I'm the strong, dominating man and she's the weak, feeble-minded woman. And it felt good, because I don't get a chance to play that role too often. So I just let her have it: "I'll never see you again. Get out of my life. Walk home. Get out of here." I was physically pushing her away from me. I pushed her away and I split. I got on a bus and I went back to my place. And like I just vibrated with that for about a month.

So a month passed. I began to feel nervous again, and edgy, and what have you, and so I went to one of her groups one night. I walked in and she treated me very gracefully. She had recovered a lot of her cool and integrated me back into the group. Only this time it was like something special. Because I was sure I knew her in a way that nobody else in the group knew her. So although she was treating me like the others, clearly I had a special privilege. And I began going

back to the group and within a few weeks I had become the
star. Everyone picked up very fast that she deferred to me in
certain ways. They thought that she was deferring to me because I knew more about therapy and psychology. And she
was deferring to me because I had the goods on her.

So the group got very, very strange. And then one night she
came up to me after the group and said, "How'd you like to
be my assistant?" I was very flattered. I was getting a B.A. in
psychology and I thought, "Wow! I'll become a psychotherapist."

I had no notion in my mind that I was too neurotic to put
on my shoes, much less become a psychotherapist. I thought,
"Fuck, if she can be a psychotherapist, I can be a psychotherapist." So she began training me. And then a new phase
began.

I began seeing her in group, where I would lead the exercises in the beginning. Then I began seeing her privately
where I became her colleague. And we began doing—it
wasn't "therapy" anymore—it was called "research." We
were researching therapeutic methods with each other. When
she got the idea to start her psychological research institute
she decided that I would be the president of it and she would
be the director, and we would gather our disciples around us.
So not only would we have the halt leading the blind, but the
halt and the blind were now going to gather other disciples
to the flock. And then it got very strange. It got very strange.

I graduated from college and had my B.A. and now began
studying for my master's in psychology. So I was really becoming a psychologist, right? I was getting the credentials and
all. And I was going part-time to school, so she paid me a
salary as her research assistant. I began to spend most of my
time there, and it began to mingle. It became research, it
became therapy, it became work, it became life. Our lives
began to be intermingled. And we began building a library.

We really discovered Reich. We discovered Laing.* We discovered all the other little crazy foundations around the city.
People who were doing ass-hole therapy and nose therapy and
all the funny therapies that are around. And we began making the scene; me and Susan would go to all the different
groups and bring the groups to us. And she and I began to
really freak out with each other.

A typical session would be—we'd have the day free. And
we'd lock ourselves in, into this big room, pull down the
blinds, lock the doors, right. And of course the atmosphere
immediately became charged and tense. Maybe we'd start off
something crazy, like, we heard that orgone energy** was
blue, and you could see it through blue cobalt. So we'd buy
cobalt-blue bulbs and get naked and fill the room with cobalt-
blue light and try to find each other's bioenergetic aura. In the
process, of course, we'd begin to feel each other up and get
closer. And the next thing you know we'd be fucking. And
we'd finish fucking, and at the end of fucking I would be
disgusted because I had been sucked in again by the spider
lady. And I would start laying some shit on her and she'd tell
me to lay down and start doing therapy on my head (fantasies, and asking me about my grandmother and all that shit).
Then the phone would ring and I'd answer the phone and
suddenly I'd be the secretary to the psychologist at the institute and I'd have to do some kind of business.

Then we'd leave and then her patients would come. And
when she was with her patients I was next door typing up
records of therapy she did with other people. It got to the

---

* Ronald D. Laing, a radical Scotch psychiatrist-author questions the entire notion of "madness," and believes that it is more helpful for a pre-
cautiously balanced individual to go completely mad in order to regain his
sanity than it is to try to control or hide his madness.
** Orgone energy refers to Reich's conception that the body discharges
invisible but definite energy waves that are related to the person's state of
mental and biological health.

point where I didn't know which finger was up whose ass-hole, when. It just became a great big boiling mess. We really freaked out.

At that point, this crazy Communist that I was living with earlier came back into my life and came to the institute and wanted to make it a Marxist organization, for the therapeutic release of the working class. So he brought that whole slob of insanity into the scene. Then he became her new darling boy, because he came on very strong and she started making it with him. So in retaliation, I started making it with her patients, drawing them away from her and making them my patients. I reached the point where I had about twelve chicks and one fag who were all my patients, and she got all the fatties and the crazies and the ones who weren't very exciting.

It was like a Grand Guignol. We were doing therapy warfare with each other. She rented the apartment next door. And we'd lead groups at the same time; she'd do her group and I'd do mine. Afterward we'd meet and we'd rap about each other's groups and find out that psychic waves or something was passing through. Because while I was having dinosaur fantasies going on in my group, she was having cave man fantasies going on in hers. Then we started doing energy experiments, where people would lay with their heads on each other's crotches and try to figure out whether the other person was giving or sending energy or transmitting or what they were doing with it. We tried to set up controlled experiments, which didn't work because we couldn't control the thoughts. And then we took off into the parapsychology crazy wing and we got involved with all the parapsychologists who started coming in.

At this point I was functioning absolutely brilliantly. I was keeping twenty balls in the air at the same time, but I was totally unconscious and completely neurotic. I was fucking anything that came into sight. Anything that seemed interesting I would dive into and Susan would be right around the corner. We were like two dogs sniffing at each other's shit piles, trying to find out who had the most interesting thing going. In a sense it was the most therapeutic thing I could possibly imagine, because I involved myself in extraordinary relationships with human beings that went beyond any conventional sense.

At one time the Communist crazy and I and Susan had an orgy, which ended up with him putting me down for fucking his wife, and I was telling him that I only fucked his old lady because I loved them both. And while we were discussing that in a Marxist context, he was fucking Susan in the ass and she was sucking me off. So it got very very far out. And we were doing things that normally would have freaked me out if I began to understand what I was doing. So it was like a lot of experience and no awareness.

It just got sicker and sicker and sicker until it reached a point where I couldn't take it anymore, and one day I just walked out and said, "It's stupid. I quit." And I walked out and spent the summer up north.

I came back that fall and got a job as an editor and only began to see Susan socially. She would have a party or I'd drop by to see her and we'd rap. We became friends in a strange sort of way; people who just knew each other very well but didn't have much to do with each other. It wasn't until about three years later when I dropped acid and I began to flash my whole life, that the entire incident came back and I said, "Oh shit. Is that what it was all about? Is that what we really did with each other?"

We lived through that entire cycle with each other totally spaced—with no sense of what we were doing. And all the while we were calling it therapy.

In the context of my other therapeutic experiences it was the best and the worst. It was the best because she (more than any other therapist I've ever been in therapy with or ever seen) was willing to dive totally into the basic experience and really live it. The beautiful parts of it were when I was having fantasies that were so far out and working physically at the same time. She would spend hours working with me, making sure I wasn't copping out, that I would explore every last avenue of the fantasy before she would stop. I mean a session with her was theoretically fifty minutes, but it could last two or three hours. If it really got going she wouldn't stop. She was really concerned that the patient got what he needed at the time.

She stumbled on to the marathon theory before people were into marathons. She didn't have the vocabulary, so there was no sense of what it was. But she understood very early in the game that when it really gets going, if the clock says fifty minutes, fuck the clock. It's the human being that's important. So I learned this from her. All the therapists I've known and seen since then who do this—"Well, your hour's up and you're in the middle of your most cataclysmic insight, but that's too bad. Life is practical and really we have to get on to the next one."—I've seen that as absolutely total bullshit since then. I understand the reason of it: it's cool. But I'm not going to do this scene. Because if the clock is more important, why bother with the therapy in the first place?

Susan was also the worst because the thing I needed most I never got from her. The thing I needed most was limits. I needed somebody there who would give me limits that I could define myself against. Because at that time it was all primary process. It was all just pure schizzy stuff, flowing out, flowing out, flowing out. And what I needed was an occasional guidepost so I could say, "Oh, in relation to that set of values or that context, this is where I'm *at*." Which is not to say that this is what I *am*, which is the analytical mistake—you analyze it, you define it, and that's what you *are*. Horseshit. That's where I'm at in relation to something. She never gave me anything to be anything in relation to.

So it was incredibly liberating and at the same time compounded by confusion. I will say this: it drastically altered the course of my life. For better or worse, I don't know.

Simultaneously, as I was beginning to see her, there was a professor of psychology who was the head of the department. He flashed where I was at and he took me into his office one day and told me that what I needed was analysis. And he knew a guy for twenty-five dollars an hour.

I said, "Wait a minute. I can't make twenty-five a month rent. So where am I going to make twenty-five an hour?" And he said, "That's too bad, because you really need analysis, right now." I said, "Well, Susan is going to see me."

"Oh, she's just an old momma," he said. "You don't need a momma, you need someone who's intelligent." And I said, "Maybe that's so, but what can I do?" And he said, "Well, too bad," in effect.

I've pondered a number of times: what if at that time I had met a strong, male, very rational analyst, who had taken where I was at that time and helped shape it? Who would I be now? It's a very freaky thought, you know, that I could in some existential sense be somebody different who wouldn't recognize who I actually am now, who would look at what I am now and say, "Who's that crazy guy?"

The effect it had on me long range was to put me on the path of coming to terms with my craziness. Because acid followed after that and Laing followed after that and the whole metatheater trip—the trip of living out your condition, whatever it is. Even if it puts you in front of a firing squad or an insane asylumn, be who you are. And that's how my life has developed. So I guess she was absolutely crucial in helping me to make me who I am.

Whether, in any traditional sense at all, what she did could be called therapy, I doubt. But what else would you call it?

Which gets into the question of what is therapy, anyway?

I've had other therapeutic experiences. One was Harry, a Gestalt therapist, trained by Fritz Perls.* I saw him for about four months. About three years ago. I stopped seeing him when I dropped acid. I saw him just prior to my first acid experience. I was in one of my usual my-life-is-falling-apart periods. I was holding down a job which I didn't like. And I was getting involved with Karista,** and a bunch of free-love people and communitarians. I had this notion that I wanted to go live on a farm. I had this notion that the communal life was the only true life: Western civilization was finished. And I was simultaneously seeing a Gurdjieff guru,*** who was like laying incredibly heavy trips on my head. Anything I said that was other than pure description, she said, was pathology. To her all of Western psychology was trivia.

So I didn't know where I was because of so many heavy influences that were coming down. And I met this chick and she said to go see Harry. And all Harry did was I would go there and I would rap with him and I would like get into my trips and he would tell me things about myself from time to time. But basically he would say, "You're forgetting to breathe." He'd say, "You have to remember to breathe because if you don't breathe, everything else is silly." That was his one trip. And his other trip was he would laugh at me. I would come in with some incredibly cataclysmic story. I'd get all wound up in the melodrama and wait for sympathy, and he would laugh and say that's the funniest thing he had ever heard.

---

* Frederick Perls, M.D., Ph.D., was the originator of Gestalt therapy. This therapy is based on the idea that psychopathology consists of projecting onto others the disowned parts of one's own personality. Treatment consists of helping the patient take responsibility for his projections.

** Karista was a utopian organization that believed that the sharing of people and property led to fulfillment and happiness.

*** Gurdjieff was the Russian philosopher-mystic-holy man who taught enlightenment through detached awareness of oneself. Various of his disciples practice this art in group meetings—the process is not unlike psychotherapy in many ways.

He was gay, by the way, and at one point I put it to him. I started telling him about my homosexuality. I said, "One thing that's the trouble is that I know you're gay and I'm afraid that if I let go, we'll have sex." And he said, "Oh, I couldn't be less interested in having sex with you. I have sex with other people." So like the sex thing with him was cool. He knew it was there and he recognized it and he called it and he said, "You know, it's not going to happen. Just forget it."

He was very good for me. Good for my head. He taught me not to take myself so seriously. Not to think that because I was in the middle of a melodrama, everybody else was going to get involved in it. With Susan, any melodrama I had, she played the supporting role. With him, if my melodrama got tedious he just got bored, he laughed, or he yawned, or he said, "You're not breathing. Who's interested in your story?" So he gave me a place. A sense of perspective on myself.

But then I dropped acid. And the acid was so strong that I just had to do acid for a while. By the time I had finished doing acid, I was in New England. I finished my acid trip and I wound up in a resort up there.

I saw other therapist types, but they were more in the guru tradition, like Zen masters and that kind of trip. Then, when I came back from New England this past winter, I saw another woman—Hilda, a psychiatrist. Hilda's trip is totally eclectic. Anything that works, she uses. And she's a very strong woman. She had her leg crushed in an accident, and she spent six months in excruciating pain. Out of that she came out tested and hardened. One leg is still withered. She wears a brace on it. And her trip with me was—well, by the time I came to see her I was much more in control of myself than I ever had been. So I was able to go in and say, "Here's my problem. What can you do for it?"

My problem at the time was being on a heavy death trip. So I said, "I'm on a death trip, what can you do about it?" And she said, "I can't do anything about death, but I think if we find out about death you'll find that your real problem is life. And that's what I can help you with. I can teach you how to take care of yourself. I can help teach you how to do things so that you don't destroy yourself so much." And what she would do would be to let me talk and then she would suggest things for me to do. Physical exercises or breathing. Or she would ask questions. That therapy lasted about seven weeks, and the last two sessions were talking about sex and money.

I said, "I find you very attractive as a woman and I really dig talking to you, but I'm beginning to feel sexual attraction toward you and I feel like that's impossible."

And she said, "I never sleep with my patients. That's a rule."

And I said, "Well, that's awkward, because you know it's an artificial thing. You call it therapy but if there's a real impulse between us and you have a rule which says 'No,' I can't dig it. Where I'm at in life now there is no distinction between therapy and life. They're just different intensities but they're the same process."

And the second thing I said was about money. "I can't come here and give you thirty dollars a session and feel that you value me as a human being. If you value me as a human being, you'll see me for free; because you like me, and I'm valuable to you and because I give you as much as you give me."

She said "You're perfectly right. I have no argument with that whatsoever, but I earn my living as a therapist. If you want to see me, you'll have to pay me."

I said, "I can't fuck you and I have to pay you to see you. It sounds like an unprofitable whorehouse."

And she said again, "You're right. I can't argue with you. And if you feel that way, then you can't keep coming to see me."

I said, "Well. That's like the end of the therapy then."

And she said, "The door is open. Anytime you have anxiety or you're in trouble, give me a call and come see me."

I said, "For thirty dollars?"

"Right."

"Okay. If I'm ever in a real anxiety fit, I'll give you a call."

And we embraced. It was very warm and man-womanly. Very rich and lovely. And I left and that's been my therapy trip.

Of all my therapists I think Susan was most crucial. Not better, but more crucial. She met me at a more susceptible time and she invested more in me, even though she was doing it for her own needs. She wound up giving me immense amounts of time and energy and expertise. She was a very brilliant woman and taught me a lot about psychology and what have you. Part of my trip with her of course was coming to terms with her husband, who sooner or later got to know that I was making it with her and then I would have to see him at parties, right? And go through those changes. So like, you know, what's therapy?

If therapy is what teaches you most about life, then Susan was the best therapist, even though she was the worst because the sex pretty well tore down everything that had been built. It was very destructive. She gave me more when we weren't fucking than when we were. With the fucking came a kind of—she had me by the balls, as it were.

If I had to make a choice among the three therapists I saw and could pick out the one I would've wanted to work with when I was twenty-three, it would be Hilda. I've discovered that no matter how many trips I take inside my head, life goes on in a pretty mundane fashion. The things that become increasingly important to me are being able to have enough food and shelter and clothing and friends and loved ones. So I'm becoming increasingly sane—not through any ideological preference but just because it feels more natural to live sanely. I can be as crazy as a bedbug inside (I fantasize like crazy), but more and more important is the ability to sustain my day-to-day life.

Of all the therapists, Hilda was the one who most vibrated to that; who understood everything (all the craziness and all the trips), but who never let her attention waver from what was most important. And the most important thing is that a person be a responsible human being. "Responsible" being used in a very special sense: that a person know himself very, very, very well. And because he knows himself that well, he doesn't add to the confusion and insanity and horror that's in the world today.

So I think that if I had seen Hilda at the beginning, I would have had all the craziness anyway—because that was in me—but it would have shaped itself more sanely sooner. I wouldn't have had to exhaust myself so much. I wouldn't have had to run out to the end of the string so many times.

AUTHOR'S POSTSCRIPT

Marcus raises a very profound and perhaps unanswerable question: what is therapy? Is it a process that provides new experiences and teaches more about the ways in which life is lived, or is it relief of pain and symptoms?

His case also illustrates how a sufficiently motivated person (motivated, that is, to seek awareness and comprehension) can experience the most distressing kind of encounter—which his relationship with Susan surely was—and yet profit from it.

As far as Susan is concerned, her possible brilliance as an innovator was rendered worthless by her lack of discipline. She could not contain her own desires and persisted in attempting to get Marcus (and numerous other patients) to fulfill them. It was Susan who initiated the intimacy and Susan who terminated the treatment when the intimacy began. In neither instance did Marcus feel that the right judgment was being exercised. Susan never asked Marcus how he'd feel about these decisions before unilaterally making them, and it was only his belief in her therapeutic effectiveness and wisdom that won him over without his even voicing his doubts.

The reader may well wonder how it is possible for Marcus to be so strong and yet so weak, so chaotic and confused and yet so capable of insight. I know of no way to make this paradox more comprehensible. Suffice it to say that such contrasts represent the existential condition of Marcus's life. His chaos, confusion, and weakness caused him to seek therapy in the first place. There is little reason to doubt that he would have saved himself considerable wear and tear had he stumbled upon Hilda as his first therapist. It was only his strong side and capacity for insight that prevented his being irreparably damaged by contact with a therapist like Susan.

8

CAROL

"He couldn't get rid of me. I was always up to something."

She is a voluptuous young woman who is coy about stating her age but must be (given the age of her oldest daughter) in her early thirties, at the very least. Yet she looks a good ten years younger. Her voice is deep and coquettish.

The mother of two girls, ages fourteen and twelve, she works part-time as a girl Friday in an advertising agency and is studying for a bachelor's degree in sociology.

My first therapist was the one with whom the intimacy occurred. With the second one it almost happened again, but it didn't quite come off, fortunately.

When it all began, I had been separated from my husband for a very short time. He had been my sweetheart from very early childhood. Now I had the problem of raising the children alone—or not raising them. I really didn't know what I was going to do. I was rather confused after many years of marriage, and I wanted some help. At that point I had never known a psychiatrist nor known anything about what happened during therapeutic sessions. I had been toying with the idea only because I had heard that there was this really groovy bachelor who was a psychiatrist, who was the neighbor of a gal I knew. She did nothing but talk about him. She thought this psychiatrist was having an affair with another neighbor who was a lovely Hawaiian girl. So I decided I would go to him. He sounded like the perfect person to help me.

I was in my mid-twenties then, married for eight years, and my husband and I had just separated. And I was just confused. I didn't know how I was going to do anything by myself. I was really frightened. I had had a boy friend from the time I was six, and now I was alone.

So I called Joseph, the psychiatrist. He was on vacation, but he called me when he got back. Somewhere deep down I had this fantasy about him as a potential boy friend. He sounded absolutely exciting. I loved everything he was doing. It fit into my fantasies very well. I decided that if I were going to see anyone, it would be him. I don't know whether I wanted the help more or wanted to meet him more. I wasn't sure.

Well, I arranged an appointment with him and went to his office, which was part of his apartment. He took my history, and we talked. And I remember distinctly in the first session telling him I didn't think I was ever going to find a man that I'd be happy with. I *think* what I was emphasizing was that I didn't think the kind of man I wanted would want me. And I wasn't sure what I wanted.

During that first session he told me he didn't like my dress (not the particular dress I was wearing but the style), that my hair was too seductive, that my gait was suggestive, that I had too much jewelry on. The next time I came in I had taken off all the jewelry, the red lipstick, and did the best I could to amend my gait. It didn't help very much. And we went on like that with fairly legitimate sessions, about eight times.

During the course of the eight weeks—I guess it was about the sixth week—he told me he didn't think I had any problems that could not be solved. They were all very real. And he thought that, more than anything else, I needed a lover. That that was my main problem: I had been involved with a man from such an early age and now I was living alone and I was frustrated. After that he kept asking me if I had ever had an orgasm, and I'd say "I think so." Then I'd describe it and he'd say, "Yeah, that sounds like it," (which just amused me no end). I never talked about it myself. There was no problem about it. But he questioned me about it. And, not knowing very much and being unsophisticated, I answered.

He was an analyst. As I recall, he had two chairs in the office (I sat in one of them) and a couch adjacent to his chair.

During the next to last session I asked him if I could lie down because I didn't want to look at him. I did lie down with my head practically at his feet, facing away from him. And during the course of the session I turned and faced him. I was about six inches from his face, and I remember being terribly flirtatious. I don't know whether that's why he wanted me to stay or not. I remember thinking that. Because that same session ended in my telling him that I was having some problem paying him; that my ex-husband refused to pay and that I'd have to wait until my agreement was settled so that I could continue. He suggested that I continue with him regardless and wait to see what happened with the money.

I didn't want to do that. I didn't want to run up a bill, and secondly I really wanted to see him socially, not professionally. He was about forty at the time. He had been divorced. His former wife (I'd seen pictures of her) looked very much like me. She'd also had children from a previous marriage that were about the same age as mine were.

Well, I told him that I would think about it. I came back the following week and we talked again, and I told him that I didn't think that I wanted to continue until I knew what the elements of my money situation were. After the session he put his arm around my shoulder, walking me to the door and said,

"If you need anything, call me." I could hardly walk out of the place, my knees were shaking so much. I was tremendously excited.

Well, I left. And now I had a job in front of me. I wanted to see him socially. That was the end of the therapy and now I could have him. So I went home and that evening I called him. His service told me he was at his country house and they gave me the number. I called him there at about four o'clock in the morning. I got on the phone and asked him if he was alone. He said he was. Then he wanted to know who it was. When I told him he laughed uproariously.

I told him that I couldn't sleep, because all I could see was his face. Every line and every crease in his face was keeping me awake. And I wanted to see him. Finally he said, "Well, I'll call you on Monday when I get back to the city." He said that I was going to be back with him as a patient, and that he wanted to think about what was going on.

He did call back on Monday and he explained to me that I was involved in a transference, that it was not ethical for him to see me, that he would see me if I didn't come back as a patient and he set a time on it (I don't remember how long it was, because he said also that I'd have to be divorced. I guess he felt that I'd be going back to my husband at some point). By Friday I was absolutely out of my mind. He was all I could think about. I was determined I was going to see him that Friday whether he wanted to see me or not. I assumed he didn't have a patient scheduled for my Friday time.

So I spent the morning in the bathtub, with oils that would have drowned Cleopatra. I spent the entire morning preparing for him—resolved that he was going to see me. And I called him *after* I had called a cab, to tell him that I wanted to see him. It was pouring rain and I felt terribly cuddly and I couldn't wait until I was divorced. And I wasn't going to come back to him as a patient.

And he said that possibility existed and, again, that I was

having tremendous problems about the transference and that he'd be willing to discuss it with me and explain it to me.

I had one foot out the door and the phone rang, and he said, "I don't know if you should come here and discuss it. Perhaps we had better talk about it on the phone." I said a cab was waiting, and he said, "Okay." I jumped in the cab.

I got there and rang the bell. I was about five minutes early. He opened the door. He was standing there nude with a towel in his hand, sopping wet. He said he'd just come out of the shower and I was a little early, at which point he turned and walked back into the bedroom with the towel in his hand, and got dressed in some old army clothes.

Then he went into the office. He was standing with one knee bent over a footstool and I was sitting on the sofa. I was waiting for him to tell me why I had transference problems. Then he said, "I know everything about you. Isn't there anything you want to know about me?"

I said, "Yeah, I want to know how old you are, that's one question, and I want to know what your middle initial stands for, that's my second question."

He said, "That's all?"

"That's all I could think of."

Then there was silence and I really thought I would pass out. I never remember being so clouded in my entire life. I couldn't breathe.

And then I said, "Are you going to keep your distance? You're thirty feet from me during the entire time I'm here."

At that point he took my hand and we started to neck. And he took me by my hand and he said I'd be more comfortable inside and he took me into his bedroom—I wondered how that was telling me I had transference problems—and he undressed down to his shorts. I took off all my clothes. He made some comment about my not being inhibited and he took his shorts off.

He lay down on his bed. I bent over him and kissed his

belly, and he had an orgasm, at which point I started to laugh. I couldn't stop laughing, because I had been complaining in one of our therapy sessions that the men I knew, including my husband, would have ejaculations so quickly. He was telling me constantly that it shouldn't be that way—that's not the way it is. And here I bend down and kiss his belly and he has an orgasm.

He excused himself, saying that he was just "very, very excited" and to wait a few minutes. I remember asking him about his ex-wife, what she was like, and why the marriage ended. He said he wouldn't tell me. He would only tell the woman he married again. (I packed that line into my suitcase and used it for my own repertoire. It's saved me telling my story hundreds of times.)

We waited a while and then we screwed, I don't know how many times. But it was good. He kept telling me, "You're some woman!" He had an analytic meeting to go to. So I went on home and he left.

Well, about a week passed and I hadn't heard from him. I was going frantic. And he was in the middle of writing a paper. He publishes very frequently, and he said that he just didn't have any time and that he was just overworked, and he was rather rude. I said I wanted to see him. And he said, well, if I could behave myself I could stay there while he worked— if I allowed him to continue his work—but that he didn't know if I could do that.

So I swore I would, and I came over. I cooked, and I tried to keep out of his way. I read in the bedroom, and every ten minutes I'd pop my head into his room to see if he were done yet. I couldn't wait, and I was terribly distracting to him. And he was getting angrier and angrier. He was very irritated with himself, he told me, for allowing the whole thing to happen. He felt very guilty about it:

"It never happened before, it shouldn't happen, it shouldn't have happened, it won't happen again."

Well, I wasn't going to stand for that. I had made up my mind that I wanted him on some level. I didn't know how or what, but I wanted him. And I stayed over that night. And when he started work in the morning, I went home.

Somehow, we kept some contact for that year. Each time I saw him he told me that he felt guilty and that he couldn't see me. I'd see him once a week, sometimes every other week, sometimes twice a week, most of the time at my initiative. He would always say "No" first. That was his first sentence, "No." And then I'd cajole a bit and he'd say "Okay." He was just terribly sadistic, I felt. My friends looked at it that *I* was the sadistic one, I don't know—it was a beautiful Martha-George relationship.*

At one point I thought I was pregnant. And I was absolutely delighted. I didn't want to see him any more when I thought I was pregnant. I just told him about it, that I was pregnant, and that was all. That I was going to have the baby. I was going to have his baby and I really didn't care if I saw him again.

At first he didn't believe it. Then his very closest friend picked up on it and he believed it. After they discussed it I guess Joe believed it too. Then he didn't stop calling; it just didn't end:

"You can't have that baby—you're going to ruin two lives, three lives—I'm never going to see you if you do that—I'm never going to come around—I'll send you a check every month, but I'm never going to come around." He tried and tried and this went on for weeks and weeks. And I was having the baby no matter what.

Well, I guess the most important part of this is that during the year I was seeing him I was also seeing another man,

* A reference to the constantly fighting, teasing, sadomasochistic, topsy-turvy relationship of Martha and George, the protagonists in Edward Albee's play *Who's Afraid of Virginia Woolf?*

Peter, who was very much in love with me. He had known me while I was living with my husband and as soon as I left my husband he left his wife. And he wanted to marry me. I used to see him perhaps four or five days a week. He didn't know what was wrong or why I had lost interest, but his whole life revolved about me and there was nothing he wouldn't do for me. In a way it was a story-book kind of romance, but actually he was insane.

He was determined to find out what was going on—where I was the evenings that I wasn't home, why I'd lost interest in him. I had detectives following me. And finally one day he caught on. He knew about my initial therapeutic session and he finally made the connection. Without my knowledge and much to my dismay, he began calling Joe and threatening his life and told him that if he didn't stop seeing me he was going to kill him.

I don't know what the conversations were really like. I never told Joe about Peter. I only heard from Joe later that during this time he thought that I had something to do with it. Apparently Peter was telling him that if he didn't stop seeing *that* woman (without identifying me), Joe wasn't going to live. And he knew exactly where Joe was every minute of the day. As soon as Joe walked into his house—either his vacation retreat or his city apartment—Peter would call. It was really getting bad. It went on for about three months.

Finally Joe called the police. He was really frightened. The guy was flipped. He really was going mad. And the police called me. I was at my parents' house when they called. Joe had tracked me there.

So the police get on the phone and they tell me the whole thing, that Dr. Joe is down at the precinct and there's a complaint that I have been threatening his life. Threatening his life? This was about ten months into this ridiculous relationship. And I was furious.

How could he implicate me? First of all, I didn't know anything about it. This was the first I had heard. I called Joe later. I was just—I was so angry.

He holds an administrative position in one of the large hospitals in the city and when I had told him off, I called the director of his hospital and I told him the whole story. Joe was called down and there was a tremendous to-do. He was pleading with me and it was just an absolute mess. At which time he sent me a letter rescinding his statement to the police. He was, I guess, afraid of losing his job. And here I am pregnant. It was really a mess.

Well, then I found out I wasn't pregnant. That was the first time that my period had been delayed in my entire life. It had been regular every twenty-seven days to the day for my entire life. And here I was, it was really a pseudocyesis,* because I had all the symptoms, everything. I was swelling, and just everything which I actually had during my real pregnancies.

I didn't tell Joe I wasn't pregnant, though. He continued to think I was. The third month was approaching and he was dying. He was pulling the hair out of his head. He would call me I don't know how many times a day, begging me to do away with the baby. He said if I did, he would do what I wanted, on my terms.

Finally I said "Okay, you find a doctor."

And he said, "No, you find one."

We argued about every little point.

Well, I don't know why I ever let him off the hook. He didn't really deserve it, but I went ahead with my false abortion. I couldn't at this point tell him that it wasn't really so. And I wanted him to suffer. I was still incensed at his calling the police and all these machinations. He just assumed it was me, that I was the one. Which was true, but I wasn't making

* This refers to a false pregnancy with all the symptoms of a real pregnancy.

the calls. He could've consulted me, and it would have certainly helped. I wasn't up to murder—quite. Maybe torture but not murder.

And even before that episode I was angry with him. I couldn't have what I wanted. I was angry that it wasn't the kind of relationship that I wanted; that he wasn't in love with me, that I was having such a hard time with it. That I had to beg practically to see him each time. It was a little game he had arranged—we had both mutually arranged—and I didn't like it. So I fought, I was really grooving on it. I wanted to change it, but he wouldn't have anything to do with that.

So I had this false abortion. He disappeared at the time I was having it. It turned out that he had gone to his house in the country.

He never pretended to care for me more than he did. At one point he hit me in the head with a cane. I was such a pest. He had been in a car accident and he was really hurt and he hadn't slept in days, and his beard had grown. And he was weary and he had seen patients all day. I wanted to see him and he said "No" and I said, "I want to see you," so I went over.

I knew his schedule well and so I knew when I could come in. He had a group at that point, so I just floated in with the group and sat in the waiting room. He couldn't get rid of me. I had told him on the phone that if he didn't see me I was just going to go in the bedroom, take off all my clothes and throw myself out the window. I was always up to something. So I went in and I waited till it was over and he put me in his bedroom. He didn't want anyone to see me sitting out there.

He was very secretive about his past; about his ex-wife and about his mother in particular. So here I was in his bedroom for two hours with all kinds of file cabinets. By the end of the two hours I knew everything about his past, including where he had his religious confirmation. I just knew everything. And what I didn't know, I found out after that from the clues I had uncovered in the files and the pictures I had seen and the letters I had read.

So I was there and he was totally exhausted. He sat down in his chair with his newspaper and he was screaming at the top of his lungs that he was helping people all day and he was tired of being with people. Not that he doesn't like helping people, but he's not going to do it anymore that night and he wants to be let alone and I'm intruding on his privacy. And he's screaming like an absolute maniac. At which point I got up and threw myself at him—crashing into his newspaper— and started biting his neck. He was really stimulated and he just sat on the chair. I pulled his slacks off and sat at his feet, stimulating him more. Every time he was about to have an orgasm, I'd stop. And he'd scream, "You bitch!"

We'd go on like that for about an hour. Finally he said to me, "Not like that," and he took everything off but my sweater.

And I said, "Not like that."

And he said something again like "You bitch!", and then I started running around the room and he was running after me. It was really turning into a tremendous fantasy I was acting out—a whole rape thing.

Finally I was just lying naked on the floor and he said, "You'd make a great picture." I told him he could take the picture if he promised to look at it every day. He laughed, got dressed, and said he wanted me to leave. That second. There was no staying over. There was no talking about it. He was tired and he was going to sleep.

But I wouldn't go. He began to yell. Then he took the cane he was using and he just hit me over the head. So I sat on his doorstep for a couple of hours, until he finally pacified me and I went home.

After I had the "abortion" he wouldn't sleep with me any- more. He didn't trust me. He said I had stopped taking birth control pills, and even if I was taking them he didn't know that I would keep on with them.

But he would see me. We'd go for a walk in the park or we'd go to the museum. He had agreed that if I had the abortion we'd have a "new" kind of relationship; he would be "good" and do what I wanted. I thought he would do anything I wanted him to do, but he wouldn't sleep with me. Well, this wasn't what I wanted.

So we met in public places only. He wouldn't see me alone, because he knew that each time he'd told me he wouldn't sleep with me, we ended up doing it anyway, so he said it had to be in a public place. He arranged for us to meet in the hospital lobby or something. Once we got into a conference room at the hospital and there was a narrow doorway. He was standing in the doorway to let me through. We sort of brushed next to each other and he just ran away, fast. It was an incredibly exciting experience for both of us. We talked about it very often. It really was super-stimulating.

I knew where he was all the time. I was constantly following him around. I would always show up at meetings he was at—drive him nuts. Everybody I knew was involved in it and my girl friends would go if I couldn't go. He'd always see the front row filled with my friends. He talked frequently. He was a very big talker.

Then finally when I realized that he really wasn't going to sleep with me, I didn't want to see him anymore. I just stopped. I said, "Forget it. This is not for me." All the fun was out of it. That was really what I wanted. I didn't want any kind of relationship with him and I didn't realize it until this happened. I had decided before I met him to sleep with him and when he didn't want to anymore, it was all over. I haven't seen him since.

I went back into therapy about two and a half years ago with somebody whom I really adored. I did extremely well with him for about a year. I had been dating someone for three years and I was miserable about it. It was a real see-saw thing. When I wanted to get married, he didn't want to. When he wanted to get married, I didn't want to. And I was very much in love with this man for years, and I needed some help in deciding what to do. Either I was going to shit or get off the pot. So I went to another psychiatrist, Edgar, and he was very helpful.

At the end of about eleven months with Edgar I told him that I didn't think there'd ever be a man that I'd care about again and there was nobody that I would go near physically. He said facetiously that he was going to take my private bodily parts and wrap them up and put this man's name on it and throw them out the window. And then I yelled at him. He was sitting next to me on a couch and he threw me over his lap and started to spank me. And I said if he didn't stop I was going to rape him. And so I looked up at him. It was the last thing in the world I had thought of. He was always my mother. That was my transference.

But the spanking turned me on. I panicked when I felt that. I couldn't believe it. And I wasn't going to come back the following week. I skipped a session and he called me. He was really concerned. He knew about my previous encounter in all the details. In fact he knew and disliked Joe, and he was afraid that it would really get bad. He didn't want to get into any trouble. So he said I should come in, he wanted to talk to me, and I did. He told me he didn't think he could see me anymore, that he was having too many problems with his countertransference.* He had changed me so much that I had only praise for him. But he said it wouldn't work out anymore and that it would be better if I saw someone else. Which I did.

Now I'm seeing somebody who's very classical. I found this Freudian analyst on my own and see him once a week. I felt

* This refers to the analyst's acknowledging that he is too emotionally involved with his patient to work objectively with her anymore.

that I should still be in therapy, although I didn't know what my problems were. I only knew that I didn't have any specific goals in my life and I felt that I should have some. And in the last year, since I've been with this doctor, I have a whole new idea of what therapy is about.

Considering where I had been when I first separated from my husband, in terms of sophistication, knowledge about life, Joe probably gave me the most tremendous impetus that any person I've ever met has given me. Impetus to move, to change my life from living in a cloistered shell, going from my parents' home to marriage at an early age—not really knowing what was happening in the world. I took up many of his interests. I got very interested in psychology. I vacationed where he vacationed. I took up the sports that he liked. I would probably rank him number one among my therapists.

If anything, the intimacy added to things. At one point four months after I started seeing him socially, he really decided that it had to end. He was going crazy. He couldn't sleep. He was guilt-ridden. He sent me a bill (I have a collection of bills and letters from him, sometimes I think of mailing them to him). He absolutely would not have been more helpful to me if he'd resisted and didn't screw me, because I was not prepared for therapy. I had no motivation to work in therapy. I just didn't know enough to understand the process. But this actual acting out and this living experience was dynamic for me, in terms of change that occurred in me.

I started to see his world, and I liked it. I was very discontent where I was. I didn't like the way I was living and I didn't understand why. I just knew that I was not happy. I didn't know why. Spending time with Joe made me see what I wanted, and I went in that direction very quickly. It was a tremendous break to leave the middle-class suburbia that I'd belonged to and been bred in, and to venture out on my own. If I hadn't met Joe I probably would have gone back to my husband. I would have stayed in the middle-class, unpsychoanalyzed environment. It would have been the same Sunday dinners at my mother-in-law's house, where everyone was teased to the top.

So my scope broadened tremendously. I'd lived in a very montonously routine life style with very few opportunities open for anything more to happen. Now I feel I've matured.

That was the positive part of the experience with Joe. I was forced to grow up very quickly. I was really a very little girl when all this happened. I was a child. I was rather retarded for my age in terms of social development. And it really shook me up. It pushed me ahead very quickly. It compensated for all the years I'd been stagnating. Unfortunately, along with the growth there was a lot of pain. And I saw that life was not all roses. Making me adjust to that, and learning that not everybody can love you, and that not everyone is going to pamper you, was rather shocking. I lost my equilibrium for a long time.

It left me at loose ends. But I had started in a labyrinth. And I had taken all the loose ends and I had gotten out of the cave. And there I was, out of the cave in this big world. But I had managed to get out. I don't know that I would have done it otherwise.

AUTHOR'S POSTSCRIPT

This is almost a reverse situation of Marcus's affair in terms of who drove whom crazy.

While I find scant evidence to validate the usefulness of this experience for Carol, still there is no indication that it was harmful to her in any way. That of course wasn't the case for her suffering therapist.

Joe evidently read Carol correctly in realizing that she wanted an affair more than she wanted therapy. But he was obviously unwilling to offer her anything more than a one-night stand. He missed the boat in not realizing the fury of a Carol scorned.

For this reluctance to offer a continuing man-woman relationship he paid dearly. If he had never been intimate at all or if he had surrendered more fully to the affair he would likely have experienced less grief. I suspect his guilt over having slept with a patient prevented this latter course of action.

Some may read this story as a morality play: Joe played with fire and had his fingers burned. I would read another moral into it—one based on Joe's ambivalent attitude toward his intimacy with Carol: He who vacillates is lost.

9

BARBARA

**"I was detached when I started and no better at the
end"**

*A twenty-five-year-old concert musician, she is moon-
faced, pretty, but a bit on the plump side. She wears a blue
pants suit and has a far away look in her eyes.*

*She speaks in a slow, soft voice, barely audible at times,
and long, silent stretches go by between statements. She is in
poor eye contact with me, preferring to stare into space.
There is a lost, detached quality about her. Much of the information that follows had to be drawn out by constant ques-
tioning.*

I saw my first therapist during my freshman year at college.
I just wasn't functioning. I was exceedingly depressed and
suicidal. Therapy was the only viable alternative at that
point.

I was not able at all to relate to anybody, to go ahead and
do my work. I was with the symphony orchestra in a city in
Connecticut and that was very difficult to contend with. I
couldn't even play. I'd been with the orchestra since junior
high school. After high school I came to New York to study
and work. And then I decided to go back to Connecticut and
go to college. I was really fucked up. My whole sense of

anything was just fear. And I just couldn't move. I was isolated and had no girl friends or boy friends.

So I would go over to Student Health to see a guy once a week. And when the term was over, he suggested that I continue. I had a consultation with two psychoanalysts he suggested and my folks chose Ted. I saw him about three or four times a week for about two years.

I don't really know how to describe therapy with Ted. From the first meeting he was very nice and unpushy and gentle. And I was scared. Of facing him and facing me. He was different, because all the doctors I ever knew were Jewish, and he wasn't. He was just rather cute and rather charming. And very warm.

In therapy I talked, sometimes I sat quietly. He wouldn't talk. I have very nebulous recollections of therapy with him. I know he paid attention to my feelings, which rather shocked me. I didn't think they were worth anything. He was the first person that I remember encountering that I felt really cared about me and accepted me, more than I did myself. He even accepted the fact that I didn't accept myself.

I used to do a lot of writing then—free associational writing. I used to send him a lot of stuff in the mail. And many times I'd pick up on very grandiose kinds of ideas: cosmic and metaphysical. That's the way I started out and he'd be pulling me back down to earth to deal with reality—dealing with issues relating to my parents.

I used to sit in a chair when I first saw him. I guess that went on for a couple of weeks. And then one day he said to me, "Next time you're here we're going to use the couch." And from there on he said he wanted to hold my hand. I know that he only wanted to make contact with me. But I was not accessible.

In the beginning I just said "No," and looked away. Sometimes he would pursue it further and try to get me to say why not, and deal with it on that level. And other times he would say, "What are you afraid of?" I was so fogged over; essentially, I was afraid of myself. I didn't see it as any sexual advance, just a desire to break through to me. But I couldn't make contact. I couldn't reach out. And I wouldn't let him reach me for quite a while. As much as I wouldn't let him, I wanted him to. And I enjoyed the fact that I could say "No" as well as say "Yes."

Later on in therapy (I'm really jumping ahead), perhaps a year and a half later, I would want him to hold me. I would say, "Hold me." And he would always say "Yes." He always wanted to. It became actually, I think, a way of hiding a lot of things from him. And a way of not dealing with a lot of issues.

I used to hold his hand quite a bit, once I was able to. And then he would sit on the couch and I would sit next to him and he would hold me.

When I'd ask him to hold me, I'd be feeling scared and alone. And when he'd hold me I still felt scared and alone, but I felt better. I think I wanted to keep things like a child being comforted by its mother, but I started growing up. It was very confusing there for a while, because I didn't know what I wanted. I felt very funny at times. And we didn't talk about it. I didn't deal with it really at all.

I felt funny because then I would want to kiss him and he would kiss me, and we would kiss each other and embrace. I wasn't sure if I was a child kissing a mother or a father or a friend, or a woman kissing a man. I didn't know what I was. And things could have precipitated a lot farther a lot sooner as far as what was going on—as far as actually making love. Because there was a sense of intimacy between us.

I was afraid to initiate kissing. I wanted to kiss him on his lips, so that he would kiss me more like a lover. My father didn't kiss me like that, which really confused me because I always thought I was still a child, and I could be safe hiding behind that. And I wasn't.

I couldn't think of him as being hung up on me because I didn't think that *anybody* could be hung up on me. The very fact that anybody should care about me was incredible. Me? Why waste your time? If anything, that was the sense I got from Ted. Because I thought a lot of him as a person and I didn't get the sense of him being hung up on me at all. What I got was the sense of someone *caring* about me. And I was honestly able to accept it.

After I had been in treatment with him for about a year and a half, I moved back to New York to play, practice, and audition. But I went back to Connecticut quite a bit to see Ted, because as a person I was not happy.

At one point I had mentioned going into therapy in New York. I don't know if he just gave me a noncommittal answer, leaving it for me, or if he said "No" at this point. But I assumed he said "No." I'd come to his office and we'd talk about what I was doing and how it was going. We'd rummage over photographs if I had a picture. Or he'd suggest alternatives for me to do. Or what he was doing (he was teaching then and into some courses). He'd always hug me and kiss me before I left, as a way of saying good-bye. As time went on, it just became more and more social. We'd go out for a walk sometimes, but we never went out per se.

Then—this was already after I had been in therapy for about two years—I went in one time and just said, "I want you to make love to me." It came out. I was just talking and I really didn't expect him to. I had a boy friend at the time. I felt very good about myself and I was working and I liked the work I was doing and I enjoyed my boy friend who was married (wow, the whole way I dealt with people! It was very protective; that my boy friend was married and was also not too involving.).

He did a triple take.

He said (this was very funny): "Do you feel this way often?"

And I said "Yes."

And he said, "Do you like men to make love to you?"

And I said "Yes."

That question had never come up during all the two years —whether or not I liked men making love to me. And then he proceeded to make love to me, to caress me, to undress me, to hold me. It was delightful, it was marvelous. I enjoyed it. I was glad. I was happy.

And that's about it. I got dressed and I don't know if I acknowledged what I did. I was trying to figure out where I was, in terms of my detachment. I felt good, I think he felt good, but a little funny.

I don't think it was what he expected to happen either. Because he said to me, "In retrospect, in looking back on the whole therapy, it changes a lot of things."

I asked what, but he went on to something else. That rather surprised me because I knew what was happening. *All right, I did.* I knew this undercurrent was going on, and I was rather surprised that he wasn't aware of it. I was terribly aware of it. I wanted him to make love to me, knowing that he wanted to. Knowing this for a good part of the time that he was seeing me. And the very fact that we didn't deal with it was because I didn't want to deal with it. I was afraid to deal with it. I thought it was so conspicuous and obvious by its absence. So when I said to him that time, "I want you to make love to me," it was my way of opening up the subject. It wasn't really meant as an invitation to an affair. It was meant as, "Let's get this out already."

So the first time it was fine, because of everything going along with me (in my life, where I was). But then it became something I didn't want, really. And I found his whole picture of me and concept of me to be rather naive. My whole lack of self-worth, my whole lack of freedom just to let myself alone and exist without having to prove something. I got the impression of a man who was just taken over by me as a woman.

He found me very charming, lovely. He loved my body, he loved the quality of me (whatever it is). But all the things I knew I wasn't dealing with, I thought for sure had to be obvious. And he didn't seem to see them.

In many of the sessions with him I'd be painfully quiet. Often I'd refuse to say anything, and I'd see how far I could take it. His whole lack of understanding about where I was made me wonder about him as a therapist. What does he deal with in his patients, if he doesn't deal with the basic ways they perceive themselves? And his lack of picking up on all my silences! Well, for Christ's sake! There's something going on behind it. And if I can't get at it, get it out . . .

A lot of times I felt that he was being as detached as I was. I got the feeling he was using me as a plaything. Even therapeutically. He liked the way it was, so it's all right even though I'm not too happy. But I don't understand a lot about how therapists work, their initiative, how much they leave off, so I don't know.

So then, whenever I'd go to his office, we'd start to talk, to chat about nothing, you know? And then we'd start to make love. He would start. I wouldn't take the initative. It was like just a game. Really a child's game. I'd let him take the initiative. My impulse was I would want to, but I'd let him take the initiative. And he would kiss me first. And he would undress me. And he would caress me and hold me. I would go to touch him and I got the feeling that he really didn't want me to. I would hold and caress him, but I got the feeling he really didn't want *me* to make love to *him*.

When I would see him, though, I wouldn't mention the unhappiness. I would tell him all the good things. I would go in there knowing I was unhappy and dissatisfied, but I would come in and I would talk about what I was pleased about. The way things were going, my job, and what I'd been doing. My secret hopes was that we'd talk about the things that were making me unhappy.

Sleeping with him didn't really make me feel better. It left me rather frustrated. He was a good fuck, but I stopped enjoying it and I stopped climaxing after a couple of months. I presumed he noticed it since I didn't respond the same. He asked if everything was all right, and I'd say "Yes" and let it go at that.

Then I was working steadily in New York and couldn't get in for quite a while. He called me to see how I was. I said I was fine and we spoke for a while.

I wasn't fine.

I had a job, I was working and externally everything was all right, but I was very unhappy.

So I wasn't in Connecticut for about three months. And then I was in to see Ted during this past summer a couple of times. And I think during that time, or by the fall, there was a decisive change for me. It no longer became important or necessary, and I became aware that what I was seeking was not there in any form, in screwing or in talking or in anything. I was seeking love, I was seeking myself.

I realized that every time I would see him it was a frustration situation. I'd go back to New York and get on the train and not be any happier. I wasn't coming back with the answers I wanted or the information I would need, the new insight, the knowledge that I would want. And my desire to just be in Connecticut with my folks waned. I just didn't want to be there as much as I had. That became boring. The whole thing became terribly boring and extraneous. It kind of all fit together.

He became in a way a diversion. Like I'd go in and see my father and Ted would become a diversion while I was there. The whole thing wasn't too realistic, to say the least. But it was important to me at that time to see my father after my mother died. To have the freedom to go in to see him.

I had had a good deal of experience with men before I slept with Ted, because I had just gone through a big fucking and sucking phase. I'd been out on the road with a couple of musicals and it was just the thing to do. It was never mass orgies, but I kept a guy around me all the time.

My problem sexually was that I'd get myself into things I didn't really want to be into, and I didn't always enjoy it. And I didn't always have an orgasm. I just found myself doing a lot of things I really didn't want to do, because I thought I had to prove something. They weren't distasteful—more mechanical and sexually uninteresting. Again I was looking for myself in the wrong place and going backwards into it.

I was in Connecticut a lot six months ago. In October when my father had an operation, I was there just about every week and I saw Ted for about three weeks in a row. Then I called him from the hospital one day and in our conversation there was really nothing going on. I don't think I wrote him after that or have spoken to him. I got a letter from him about a month ago. Chit-chat. That he's on vacation and he talked about some good books he'd read that he thought I might enjoy. And he had some pictures of me in his files. He said he was going through his files and he saw them. He spoke of me and my beauty and my realness and whatever (what he had to say about me in those terms) and just wished me a happy springtime.

He spoke about the book *Search for Self*. Again in the letter there was this singular lack of awareness of the reality of this search for myself and how fundamental it is to the way I function and exist and why I came to him in the beginning. It kind of became a hobby for him is the way I felt the letter approached it. Instead of going very much into the heart of my existence. And I have the feeling that I fooled him, perhaps, into thinking I was more together than I am.

In the same way I think I bulled myself and a lot of people into thinking, "She's right there, together, there's not a thing wrong or out of place," and I think he accepted a lot of that. It was important for me to put that across.

As a therapist he came at a time in my life when I felt like a child that more or less grew up underneath him. And I wanted to maintain that same kind of protectiveness and guidance into being a woman. I tried to do it with him as a lover, and I don't think it was successful at all. I can't evaluate the therapy too carefully because I don't have too much of a perspective on it. I was just very detached when I started and I don't think I was much better toward the end of it or going through it. There's a lot I blocked out—or it's just that it was a very self-indulgent kind of thing. I was not strongly directed in any way. I was very much indulged. At the time I accepted him as a therapist for whatever he offered me—just the sheer indulgence. As a lover it resolved nothing and it gave me nothing, essentially.

I think I'd evaluate him as a lover in the same way that I did as a therapist in that again *he* had to do something for me. I enjoyed him as a lover and whatever the relationship is and I still do. I have a great deal of feeling for him and I enjoy the feeling from him on just a people-to-people level; for what he did for me as a therapist, I suppose, or as an indulgent parent. And I don't think anything negative came out of it. It led me to question a couple of more things.

The fantasy with Ted was that he'd come to New York to see me and spend time with me here. I think the fantasy with men is just that *being with them will solve my problems, is going to make me happy*. If I'm trying to achieve something, just being accepted by them will give me the same satisfaction and also make the achievement easier, so that I won't have to work on what I want, which is a career.

But he never came in for the weekend that my fantasy required. And I never told him I wanted him to. I told him I wanted more time with him, and he said "Yes," but that was all.

I got back into therapy in New York with my current therapist in August. I was having a very rough time of it. Because of a hand injury I wasn't able to play at the time. I went to spend a weekend with a girl friend who had a house out in the Hamptons for the summer, and she had been seeing this therapist and told me about him. I was desperate and very unhappy so I went and saw him.

He's given me some more ammunition to deal with my own problems and with life. And I'm in the process of changing my whole concept of what a human being is, and what I am, as opposed to what I've always demanded myself to be. That I'm free to go ahead and pursue what I want to do if I take the rigid demands off and all my assumptions about having to be a *perfect* musician and a *perfect* woman with a *perfect* figure, and *perfect* make-up before I can go out and get the *perfect* job.

You take yourself as you are and you work with that. That's what people are. And I relate to men differently. I say "No" more often. Most of them I don't care to bother with and previously I would have, almost compulsively.

The whole approach, method-wise, is different. While Ted would sit there and let me spout out and say, "Yes . . . yes." my current therapist has a lot to say on what I bring up. Or I'll say something and he'll question the whole concept behind what I'm saying on the spot. And instead of a free association cathartic kind of therapy it's, "This is what you're telling yourself, these are the assumptions you're setting up, this is how you're preventing yourself from achieving what you want. Now get your experience with it on the outside and come back and we'll talk about the methodology and the philosophy behind it and give you the ammunition to go out and change habits."

And it's much more viable. It becomes up to me then, after a certain point of intellectual awareness, of sticking it out and deciding whether I want to stay unhappy, or making the effort to change it.

And I no longer panic or get frantically depressed as I used to or catastrophize the end of the world. Because it's no longer necessary. I no longer have to be this perfect thing and I can start building toward where I want to go. Perfectionism never came up with Ted, nor did specific technical ways of dealing with it. He indulged my general roundabout way of speaking, avoiding, going away from myself and it wasn't really what I wanted. I still do it a bit with Peter, my current therapist, because it's my whole habit and way of approaching things. But with Ted, we didn't speak at all to the point, technically: where I am as a person and my whole lack of self-esteem. It was a very emotional kind of experience.

I think Peter's therapy is the most valid in terms of helping me to achieve something in life and get over this and be happy. For the first time in about twelve years I experienced what it's like not to be depressed, and I thought, "Oh, is that what it's like to be alive!"

And I've come to see how I brought on my depressions by feeling very obligated to achieve, by appeasing my parents, having to get good grades. Never saying things that are not going to be acceptable. Otherwise I'm really awful. So right down the line. Toeing the line and doing the thing. And the tremendous amount of resentment that I'd just build up inside of me over doing this and then just push down. I still feel sorry for myself at times, quite a bit. No magic cures. But I'm breaking some of the patterns.

What surprises me is how much I didn't learn about Ted in being intimate. It wasn't useful in getting to know him better at all. It merely pointed up the unbridgeable space between us.

AUTHOR'S POSTSCRIPT

The understandableness and hazards of therapy are realized here insofar as it is very easy to see why Ted would reach out to establish contact with this unreachable girl. This reaching out served a silent satisfaction (to be babied, coddled) but was complicated by the fact that it couldn't be asked for directly. Thus, most of Barbara's activity seemed programmed to getting Ted to touch and comfort her physically. Yet on a thinking level she expresses dissatisfaction that he didn't "catch on" to her game. As if it were *his* responsibility.

For therapy to bring enlightenment, patients must assume responsibility for communicating their true feelings to their therapists. To sit back and blame the therapist for not catching their dishonesty (as did Barbara and Jessie) is their prerogative but also their albatross.

Yet I don't mean to exonerate Ted. My comments were meant to highlight Barbara's responsibility for the success or failure of her treatment.

I would guess that Ted's attitude toward sex was abnormal, for he never asked Barbara about her sexual feelings toward men until after she asked him to make love to her. And after making love to her he was unable ever to discuss it (it never ceases to amaze me that so many psychotherapists are out of touch with their own, and hence other people's, sex lives. Freud himself, the supposed sexual liberator, was remarkably inhibited. According to his biographer, Freud was a virgin when he married—at about age thirty—and ceased being intimate with his wife or any other woman while in his early forties).

Here again, Ted could no more help Barbara understand her sexuality than the halt can lead the blind.

Also, it shouldn't have taken too much sensitivity to catch on to Barbara's depression. The reaching out, the touching, even the intimacy apparently helped—but only to a degree. Ted never seemed to be able to go further than this.

After two years, if Ted couldn't catch Barbara's dishonesty he must be faulted for his lack of skillfulness. What patient tells the whole truth? What patient is able to—unless the therapist gets at the lies?

10

JUDY

"I felt that he betrayed me. My world had been shattered"

A twenty-seven-year-old brunette of medium height, buxom, wide-hipped, and Semitic looking, she is a social worker in a midwestern woman's prison. She has a pleasant but world-weary manner about her, in spite of her relative youth.

I was sixteen and was getting in a lot of trouble with the law and getting youth referral cards and juvenile bureau cards, and I was engaged in general antisocial behavior like shoplifting—just rebelling against everything. I was very unhappy and very disturbed. And I wanted to change. I felt like I was really fucking myself up. My brother (who is twelve years older than I am) had had his Ph.D. in psychology for a couple of years and he suggested that I go into therapy. And he offered to pay for it.

I wrote to a couple of agencies and analytic institutes and got back a few rejections. I finally got accepted at one of the agencies and started seeing a psychiatric social worker.

I saw him for about a year. But I didn't think anything was changing. I wasn't getting any better. I just felt confused, crazy, and was using a lot of drugs. So I stopped seeing him when I was about seventeen.

I just stopped. I got pregnant and I had an abortion. I asked him to write me a letter (I wanted a legal abortion) and he gave me some story that he couldn't help, that it was too much of a hassle. So I had an illegal abortion and I decided, "To hell with him. He's a schmuck and he'll never be able to understand me."

But my problems still remained. I felt I wanted to kill my parents. I hated them. I felt really dangerous, almost. I was just very aggressive. I used to carry a knife and I was in a girl's gang and had beaten people up.

About a year later I went into therapy again at a clinic at a training center. After about six months the therapist had to leave. Then they transferred me to someone else. And I felt I had gotten nothing. I felt like *The Frog Pond*, where this chick goes to seven thousand therapists.

By that time I felt like either no one could help me or everyone's a big shithead. So I left this clinic, because I was going to New York to live. I was twenty and had just graduated college. I was still shoplifting about one hundred dollars a week in clothing, but I never got caught. I was very good at it.

I went to New York still feeling kind of crazy. I was doing crazy things and I was going to really get into trouble, and I knew I should straighten myself out. I was stealing all the time and dealing drugs. And it got to be not ounces but kilos. And New York's very different than Illinois. It's very stiff out there. They don't play around. You don't get probation. And I was smart enough to know, like, "What the hell are you doing?" But I just kept doing it. I didn't know what I was doing. I was living with a bunch of rock musicians.

So I came back home, and about a week later my mother died. I went to my parents' old house before I got an apartment, and I felt I had killed her. She died of a heart attack. I came home very late and found her in bed the next morning, and I felt that if I wasn't so stoned or didn't get home at five in the morning, I could have done something. I called the police, and I called a friend. For some reason no one showed up for three hours. And I was sitting in the bedroom. My brother was in Florida on a vacation. I knew the hotel and I called him up, and he flew home and came over to the house with his best friend.

I thought his friend was very nice. Then the next week my brother said, "Why don't you go into therapy with John," the friend, and I said "Okay." Again my brother said he'd pay for it.

I was very depressed about my mother's dying. I had so many conflicting feelings about her.

But I've got to go back to make some sense. I had had a very happy childhood. My father was like great, my mother was very good to me. Everything was cool. But when I was ten and in the sixth grade, I began to notice that my mother was never home. I didn't think much about it. She'd say she was going to the raceway.

I saw her in the car with a guy once. I didn't think too much about it, but I asked her who it was. And she said it was a friend. About the same time I had a cold and stayed home from school. And I noticed the phone was off the hook. I put the phone back on but she said, "No, I want it left off, because people calling bother me."

I became very suspicious and very sneaky. The next morning while she was still sleeping I checked her pocketbook. I used to find money in it and perfume, and one time I found her underwear in it, and I figured she was going out. This time I didn't find anything especially, but I decided something had to be done. I was getting upset.

So I told my father: "I think Mommy's going out with other men."

He jumped up and said, "You're a liar! You're the tramp around here."

At that point I was doing no more than playing spin-the-bottle and the usual sixth-grade nonsense and I couldn't believe it. I said, "I'm not a tramp."

But from that moment on he really resented me.

It's like I brought something up to him that he didn't want to face. And nothing changed. I felt like I was crazy. She would deny it, he would call me names, but still it went on. Like she'd still go out every night, they would fight all the time, she would bring me all sorts of clothes and things (out of guilt, I felt) and say, "Don't worry about anything."

At about thirteen I became very sexy and promiscuous. I was sort of the "bad girl" of the neighborhood. I acquired one of those great reputations. I felt I was going to be just like her.

It was ten years of misery living at home. I wanted my mother to be there. She was away every night. She left me alone all the time. When I came home from school she was never there. I tried to hurt her very much. I used to beat her up. I felt terrible. I punched her in the face all the time. We got into fist fights.

I ran away, and I spent a week in the youth house. And all during that time everyone said they couldn't understand it. Like I had a genius I.Q. of a hundred and fifty; yet I hated school and wanted to quit at sixteen. I didn't want to do anything. I had big fights with my father where I'd try to knife him with a pair of scissors. Once the neighbors called the cops and the police came and said to him, "Don't you think she's too old to be beating her up?" And he said, "Call her brother, he knows everything."

My father would never take any responsibility. My brother was always the man in the house so I had all these feelings going on. I hated him for being weak. I hated my mother for cheating, lying, and then being nice. And she could be a nudge. She didn't want me to go out. I hated living home. It was just horrible.

So then, when she died, I was happy. I just felt she deserved it.

And the last bad thing that my father said to me was, "You killed her."

He got annoyed with me about something and said that.

My father had fifty thousand dollars in the bank and he was a miser. He wouldn't give a penny. I had had to work since I was thirteen. When I decided I was going to go to college he said, "Girls don't go to college."

I stole money from him. He was a bus driver and used to come home with a pocket full of change. And my mother used to cash bonds and steal money from him, too. We lived in a sixth-floor walk-up, though we could have moved to an elevator house, but he just didn't want to spend the difference.

This was the background when I went into therapy with John, my brother's friend, who was a psychologist.

It was the usual kind of therapy except he was very young and very good-looking and I had a mad crush on him. I thought he looked like Jesus Christ. He was a bachelor and had a beard and beautiful blue eyes. And I used to flirt with him, but sort of in a kidding-around way. I wasn't serious, because I wanted a good therapist, and I thought he was really good. I was in a group with six girls. And he used to encourage us to vie for his attention.

I had a lot of sexual hang-ups. Like I used to screw a lot and get very unhappy about it. And I really got turned off to men. And I thought he was helping me in trusting people and being less afraid to say "No"—like "I don't want to" or "I'm not in the mood." Not getting affection by sex. That there were other ways. I just felt better. Like I had cut down on stealing, and I went for a master's in social work and I was doing things. I wasn't so involved in crazy escapades. And I had a job teaching school. I had an apartment and a job, and I thought that my life was going along better.

So after a year of group and individual therapy once a week I was visiting a guy that lived on the same block as John. It was Saturday night and I got bored. I thought, well, I'll go take a walk down the block and say hello to John. I had a very bad cold and I remember I was feeling sick, and not particularly groovy or in good shape—not feeling well. So I went down the block and knocked on John's door.

He opened it and said, "I always imagined you would come to my house." I didn't say anything. And he said, "Come on in." We went into the living room. Obviously he had been drinking beer, because there were some beer cans around.

We rapped for a while and started kissing. And I remember saying to myself, "I don't want to do this. I just don't want to fuck him." But I just didn't say "No." I went along with it. I felt that it was just another thing going wrong.

We balled once and I was feeling really lousy. It was just nowhere.

He said, "Do you want to come up to the country with me?"

And I said "Yes."

I had so many feelings I wanted to say, but I didn't say anything else. I just was sort of down.

Then we went to the cabin he had. I wasn't dressed for the country, so he gave me a pair of shorts to wear the next day. I felt like a little boy, with these stupid shorts on, reading the paper, going through a country Sunday, feeling like flipped out, that he had betrayed me. That's how I felt—that he had betrayed me.

I didn't say anything the whole day. I was just a block. Then he drove me home. The appointment was still on for the usual hour the next day. When I got home I wrote him a letter saying, "I can't see you in therapy . . . I'm really sorry about what happened."

When he got the letter he called me up and said, "I want to talk to you about it." So I went down and the minute he opened the door, he got a nosebleed. He laid down and put ice on it, but it wouldn't stop. And he ended up in the emergency room of the city hospital with an unknown infection. He was seriously ill for about two weeks. Since it had happened just as I knocked on the door, I felt like God was punishing him. He deserved it.

I went to see him in the hospital and said, "I'm not coming back to therapy and that's it."

A couple of weeks later, talking to one of the girls in group I said, "Vicki, I have to tell you something. I really feel bad about it. I made it with John and I can't come back to therapy."

And she said, "Well, I've been sleeping with him for a year, and you should overcome that factor and come back."

And I thought she was crazy. I couldn't see how it would help.

After Vicki told me she made it with him I felt a little better. Like it wasn't just me he decided to make it with. I had felt he had wanted to hurt me. As it turned out, he had slept with every girl patient he was seeing that was pretty.

Everything fell into place after that. I had wondered why there were no men in the group, why he only say saw female patients. And I began to notice how he would sort of play one girl against the other, so that each thought she was special and wouldn't tell the others. There were like secrets going on all the time.

I decided to tell my brother so he would stop referring people to him. Because I remember my brother saying, "He works wonders with girls with your problem."

My brother had few friends and he's a strange guy himself. And John was his best friend. I guess he had divided loyalties. But being a psychologist and being a very ethical one, he had it out with John. That ended their friendship.

Afterward I felt my brother resented me as if it had been my fault that John had fucked me. Like I was the bad one. And in truth I really hadn't come on to him. I know when I do with a man.

I decided then that I would have no more therapy. I'd had it. I hated men. I just despised them. I couldn't trust them.

And I decided I was going to become a lesbian, that I could rely on women more. I always felt attracted to girls. I'm sure it all started from my father. He really turned me off. I thought all men would be really creepy and mean. So I began to have casual contacts with women—like kissing. It wasn't a dike scene. I was still fucking a lot and hating it, just turning off and not being able to come. And the minute I screwed someone I didn't want to see them. Cocks were like objects. I couldn't really get involved with anyone.

Then I met Bud. He was very nice to me. I thought he was cute. I knew I wasn't madly in love with him the way I know I feel about people. It just seemed like a way out: get married, settle down, stop running around, stop being unhappy. And it worked. I had a big Jewish wedding, we made a lot of money, and we went abroad. We just lived there for a year and it was lovely. Everything was a garden of roses.

It worked for two years. Everything was okay. Then I had Ellen, my baby. Bud worked at night. He was a reporter and worked the night shift, and I worked during the day. We rarely saw each other and I got bored at night. I had been used to going out all the time. I just couldn't see myself sitting home. So I started to flirt, casually. Then I started to sleep here and there with one or two pickups. And I felt very guilty. I felt I was going to do to Ellen what my mother did to me. It felt like a repetition, like I was reliving her life. Like I was her.

And after a while it became unbearable. My guilt feelings. I couldn't have sex with men. I would get physically nauseous. I said to Bud, "I can't have sex. If you want to go out, you can, but I feel like I'm going to throw up if we have sex." We went through six months of something like that when we decided to separate.

I got back into therapy when I split up with Bud. I saw the guy for two years. And then I stopped stealing altogether. I got caught in a boutique. I just did something I ordinarily don't do. I'm pretty sure I wanted to get caught and put an end to it already. They called the cops, and it was across the street from the city jail, and I really got scared. I was dressed well and I gave them a check and I got off with it. You know, I felt I could get away with anything really. But it scared me. I said, "I have a kid now. I really should . . ." I really don't know if it was an intellectual . . . it just stopped. It stopped gradually after that and I haven't stolen anything in a while now. Not for about two years.

I don't know if I should attribute it to this therapist. But he made me feel that I could have the kind of excitement I craved without the illegality. Like I always felt I needed more things. I had had nothing as a kid, with that miserable father. And here I was, earning and having some money.

The therapist said, "Go out and get credit cards—charge things if you feel deprived." And I began to feel that I could have the things I wanted without having to do it in a way that could get me into serious trouble.

I should mention, too, that in the second session with this man I said, "Gee, you're cute. I'd love to fuck you." And I was like really blatant in coming on. I was testing him. Because like he told me he was physically attracted to me. But he said it was more important that I be in therapy with him than he be another lover of mine. And I respect him. I still see him in group now that I'm back in Illinois. I stopped going privately, but I still see him in group.

I felt that even though I didn't come on to John that day, that people pick up in me something very evil, something bad. Men see something that makes me cheap. I guess I've always been very sexy without even trying.

I remember when I was seven years old, I had poison ivy and an uncle of mine giving me a calamine rubdown. Perhaps it was in my head but I felt like he was being a little more than uncleish with the calamine. And I just think the whole incident with John was just another . . . it wasn't any big thing that changed my life drastically. It was just another disappointment along the way. Another person who let me down or used me.

I feel that men just want to fuck, which is fine when I would just want to fuck, too. But when I don't, I want something else to be going on.

Anyway, I stopped seeing this second therapist because I went out to New York to try to get back together with Bud. He was already living there and he said, "Why don't you try coming out here. Maybe in a new city . . ." I had always said I loved New York.

I stayed out there with Bud about six months. And it just wasn't working. I made him into the good mother and father. Like he was my parents. And I couldn't have sex with him. It was like having sex with a parent. It wasn't like he was a man. He was my mother, then he was my father. He was just always good and always there, and I began to think he was weak. Like he didn't know how to handle me.

He made sexual demands on me in the beginning, and in the beginning he was very understanding. Then he got very upset and he started having a nervous breakdown himself. He'd start crying all the time. He'd tell me that he'd jerk off all the time and have fantasies. And I felt that I was fucking him up, that I was really a bad person. And he was different when I met him. I turn everyone into shit who comes in contact with me, that really loves me . . . anyone that really cares about me.

I know I couldn't spend the rest of my life with him. I was unhappy and I missed my friends. I missed Illinois. So I came back home. And I really just didn't feel I could work. I went on welfare and lived in this little ugly place in one of the shabbiest parts of town, with no toilet. I really didn't know what I wanted to do. Then I lived in a semicommune. There were many people going in and out. I just kind of liked the no responsibility. I'd always worked and I always had a beautiful home. I'd always loved my house.

After I had enough of that I decided to get a job and get

my own apartment and try getting myself together. So now, on the surface, everything seems pretty good. I have these things. But I still feel I'm ready to flip out at any time. Meaning one day just to lie in bed and not get up and not feed Ellen and go to the local psychiatric ward for their sixty-day cure, or something. Just be a vegetable.

I feel like there have been so many disappointments and unhappy things that went on, that I can't get out of it. Like I'm just going to be unhappy for the rest of my life. I'm still living in the past. I'm still wanting my father to believe me about my mother. I want my mother to give me an explanation. And I think I'm just generally pretty hostile to the guys I meet, in a semisweet way. And I'm just very lonely.

Sexually I made it with one chick this past summer while vacationing. A young girl. She picked me up. I always thought that an older woman would pick me up. This was a fantasy. So here I was, the older woman, and it didn't work that way.

It was very beautiful. And I was very turned on to her . . . her body. I remember saying, "I love you," almost immediately, where I wouldn't say that to a man. I wouldn't feel safe. And at the point I was the most physically excited I remember saying, "Gee, I wish she had a cock." You know, I like sex with men. I like it. I think it's very exciting. But it's the emotional aspect that screws me up. The sex is good. But the minute sex is over, everything else, my other things, start coming into play.

I always think that "Now they've fucked me, they don't really like me," and I become very possessive and very demanding. I'm a nudge, and guys get very turned off. And now that I have a child, I'm sure that I send out very bad signals, like, "She's trying to hook you."

Looking back on the episode with John I now think that he was a very sick guy, that it was my misfortune that he happened to be my brother's friend. And that it wasn't me, that it was pretty much him. But at the time I thought, it's me. That I did something. At this point I just feel sick of thinking to myself that I'm just there to get laid, and run around like crazy and see who I can sleep with so I don't have to be lonely that night.

I think it just happened at a very bad time. I was still involved with my mother's death, and being out of the house and on my own, and I needed someone to trust. It felt like my world had been shattered. Like there was no one else.

He lived in the neighborhood and I used to pass him occasionally. But I couldn't even look at him. We never spoke about it. And then I recently heard that John was a truck driver. I just think that he's a little nuts. He said that his therapist said that it was good for male therapists to sleep with their female patients who are having sex problems. That it was beneficial. And I always thought, well maybe I'll go into therapy with a woman and avoid the sexual thing. The transference and the things that come up.

Outwardly everything is great. I have a good job, secure. I'm going to go back for a doctoral degree in social work. I feel better with Ellen. She's the greatest kid. She's precious and beautiful and smart. And she loves her father. I feel like it's my fault. I took her father away from her. She's in school. I do the best I can. I don't go out till she's asleep—like ten thirty at night—and the house is nice. I spend as much time as I can with her. I exchange baby sitting. I have four animals in the house. Every few months Bud comes in from New York and I go there during the summers. Bud had to get away from me. I don't blame him. He loves Ellen and says he'll come back soon.

The whole question is one of ethics. If you want to really make it, you just stop seeing the person in therapy and do a social number. There's like a trust that's there. I haven't heard any person who's slept with a shrink where it hasn't left them with unhappy feelings or affected them.

When I'm with someone I really like I can now enjoy myself. It's beautiful then. When it's just a one-night thing it's
like the script is written already. It's ridiculous. And it's tragic
almost. Like that's all there is. But I don't meet people I really
like. I'm depressed a lot and it's hard for me to be light when I
meet someone. All right, I'll be happy and there are other
things on my mind. I write poetry. But I just carry the burden
of the past with me. I tried to do myself in a few times when I
didn't feel loved. Like a threatening kind of thing, like "Save
me." That's what frightens me more than anything, in effect.
When it becomes that unbearable that I'd really do it. And it
won't be to scare anyone. It's come up when someone I love is
leaving me, or breaks up, or when things seem really hopeless
and there's no out. I've turned the gas on, left the window
open, and got a headache. I knew someone was coming home.
And once I turned the motor on in a car, but I didn't know
how to do it. Even before I stared therapy with John, I swal-
lowed twenty sleeping pills.

I think things are better, but there's always that spot that's
still the same, like when I was thirteen. That hasn't changed
with all the therapy and with all my insights and whatever.

And the spot is that I'm no good.

AUTHOR'S POSTSCRIPT

Judy is a girl who can't reconcile polygamous sexuality with decency, either in her mother or herself. John's
involving himself with her seems inevitably to have contrib-
uted to her sense of badness, rather than affirming her worth-
whileness.

Judy's case highlights the therapist's responsibility toward
his patient when it should be clear that no useful purpose is
served by intimacy. In addition, judging from Judy's history,
a good deal of harm was possible. Here again the therapist
initiated the intimacy, in spite of the patient's unannounced
arrival at his home—perhaps more out of her loneliness than
anything else.

The task of her therapist ought to have been to examine why she had such loathing for her sexual self and to help her overcome this self-contempt. Whether her promiscuity was motivated by her appetites or her loneliness is immaterial, for both motivations were worthy of compassion.

The same is true of her mother's involvements. Judy gives no evidence at all of appreciating the spot in which she placed her mother when she told her father of her mother's dates. Why should her mother have confessed? Indeed, I spoke with Judy on a subsequent occasion about her mother's affairs. Mother seemed a pathetic, unattractive woman who was looking for little more than the companionship she lacked with Judy's father.

Noteworthy, too, is the fact that Judy's brother had no idea of the type of psychotherapy being practiced by John, even though John was his "best friend." This underscores the extreme difficulty in knowing what goes on in another therapist's office, regardless of how "ethical" or noncontroversial he seems. And this is true not only of nonentities or kook therapists like John. The therapists who were intimate with Beverly, Jessie, Kathy, and Carol are all well trained, competent, eminent people—widely respected within conventional psychotherapeutic circles. The same is true of the therapists of Nicholas and Gerald and Monica (in the accounts that follow).

As for John, it is a relief to know that he has ceased to practice psychotherapy.

11

BONNIE

"It was the most disgusting experience I'd had in years"

A skinny, angular hippie of twenty-six, she is dressed in slacks and a sweater, over which she wears an old vest. Several strands of beads adorn her neck. Her pale-blue, alert eyes highlight an unmade-up face. She works on occasion at odd, menial jobs, earning just enough money to supply her minimal material needs.

When I was about twenty, at college in Massachusetts, I started hanging around with other psychology majors and people who had been in therapy for quite a while. And I would always say things like, "Well, I'm very happy with my life because I've really gone through a lot of good changes relative to where I was last year or the year before, and I'm really happy with the progress I've made so far, and I don't feel as though I need therapy." But I had friends who would say, "That's just a copout. You really need therapy and the reason you're not going is because you're afraid to go any further, because you've reached a stage and you keep justifying that stage by saying, "Wow, look what I've already done." So if that was true I said, "Okay, maybe you're right, man. I'll go and find out."

So I went to the school therapist and he said, "Why are you here?" and I told him. He said, "Well, then there is no sense in your coming to see me because if you feel that you're all right, I don't need you with this kind of motivation." So that was just one session and I didn't go back.

Then I had this little affair-type thing with this chick who lived around where I lived and she was getting a divorce from her husband at the same time—or something like that—and she wanted to go to a therapist. She was freaking out. And so I said, "Well, I'm going to try again because this is kind of heavy and I really don't like myself for getting involved with you, and I'd really like to change all of this." So I tried another therapist. And I hated him, man, from just those first two minutes I was with him.

He was a very old German Jew kind of guy and he sat there with a notebook and he never looked into my eyes. All he said was, "Vell, vat time ver you born and vere ver you from and at vat age did you start the sexual ting, did you ever vet the bed?" He was like a robot, and I just couldn't make relating to him at all. When I left I said, "No, it's not time, because I just can't make that scene."

So then I took a graduate course at school. It was on the emotionally disturbed child, and the teacher who was supposed to teach it didn't show up. So we had another professor I really dug. His name was George and he was a psychiatrist. I dug his ideas and his whole rapport with the class. And so it happened that most of the students, because of the nature of the course, were teachers doing brush-up work. So I was one of the younger generation. The old mothers who were there weren't very aware and very hip to a lot of new things that had been happening in relationship to psychology. So the prof really had to explain an awful lot to them. I didn't have so much difficulty because I was already familiar with these things and I think he kind of liked me.

And one day I was in the middle of a statement and he

said, "Why such and such?" And I said, "Because it's obvious, blah, blah blah." And right in the middle of the statement he looked at me and said, "You're a very talented young lady."

And it just took my ego away. I said, "Wow, I really like this guy and it's really groovy."

We had a term paper due, and I had been thinking about asking him if I could go into therapy with him, because I felt as though I liked him enough that I could get into a therapy situation with him, where with the other people I couldn't. So I went one night to turn in my paper. It was due before he left the city and he was in his office in the clinic he worked in. So I brought my typewriter because I was behind schedule. And I sat down and I'm typing and I gave it to him and asked him if I could start therapy with him. And without announcing it, the therapy session started right then.

He shot me down for sitting on my ass on the floor like a little girl, typing. I· don't want to grow up. And whatever he did to my mind, when I went home that night I couldn't sleep. All night long I was . . . nightmares, phew, a real bad scene. So I thought, "Wow, this is going to be heavy. A really good therapist. He really knows how to get to the nitty-gritty." Somehow he really affected me.

So then I went to him for about three months and then I graduated. And then I wanted to go on a vacation, so I went to the Caribbean, and I lived there for about a year and some months. And I came back to the city and I called him up and said, "I'm ready to resume therapy. I took my thing, my escape from education, and I'm back again." So I started therapy again with George. This was in December of nineteen sixty-eight. And after a few months I said that I wanted to sleep with him.

So he said, "Well, I can't remain objective and be your therapist and still go to bed with you. Either I'm your lover or your therapist, what do you want?

And I said, "I need a therapist. Too bad. Forget the other scene."

So at first I was really shot down by it. Not shot down, but I was like angry. I was angry that he wouldn't sleep with me. Because my best girl friend had slept with her therapist, and there was no big thing about it. She slept with him, and it was over with, and they never did it again, and she dug it. She got something out of it. It wasn't especially sensually, erotically exciting, it wasn't the best lay she ever had, but it was enjoyable. She learned a great deal from it, she claims. I never went into the details with her because she was a little up-tight about it.

So one night, I was on my way over to George's place and I had this whole premonition that I would go there, we'd go for a drink to a nightclub and then we would go to his pad. I had this whole premonition on the way over. So when I got there I didn't say anything about sex. Except that he turned around to me and he said, "I want to talk to you about something."

"Yeah, I know already. I had a premonition on the way over."

"What?"

"Go ahead."

"I've been being dishonest with you. I'd really like to sleep with you. And for me to pretend that it's not important to me, that I'm still maintaining my objectivity, is a lie. So are you still interested?"

"Yeah, sure," I said. "Now I'm extremely up-tight this very moment but I'm not going to back out."

And so we went and had a drink and we went to his pad and it was the most disgusting experience I had had in years.

He had worse problems than me sexually. I think that I've always been—well, not always, I was a great pretender at one time—but I was a much better lover than many, many people. And I have been for quite a while. Like most guys usually say, "Wow, you really had a good time. Like you're really very exciting." This kind of a thing. But at the same time I'm into a homosexual thing. And that was what I was trying to get out of at the time. And I was using therapy as a means to do it.

But he had his own sexual problems, which he never told me about or never admitted to. And even at the time would not really admit them. He couldn't erect and he told me that it was always this way the first time with a new chick. So, "Have patience, come back." And then he's into S and M (you know, sadomasochism) and I still have on my breasts two scars from his fingernails.

But I went a second time to sleep with him. And the second time wasn't very good either, so I didn't see him any more in the office.

He said, "If you want to sleep with me, I'm not going to have any more over-the-desk relationship with you. I'm going to have a different kind of relationship. Maybe if you get to know me on this basis, maybe you'll get some real sense of a man, or more therapy out of it. Maybe it will be more realistic."

But I said, "I'd rather see you over the desk, because, uh . . ." I really wanted to tell him that I wanted to puke, but I had difficulty really being honest with him. Telling him he was a bad lover and he had fucked up. He was worse off than I was.

I felt really funny telling him that. Because all this time I had trusted him, looked up to him. And I never thought, never dreamed he would have this kind of a problem. And so as a result of that I was really up-tight and I just couldn't say to him what I really wanted to say to him. Because it was shooting down something I had had a lot of faith in and was using as a crutch.

I used to say to myself, "Oh he's really so together."

It's very difficult to say what the therapy was like. At the time I had one feeling about it. And now I have a different feeling about it. Now I think that absolutely nothing happened and that it was a lot of bullshit, but at the time I thought it was worth it. Because I was having a relationship with another chick, Jane, who I was living with (I met her in March of sixty-nine) and she moved in with me.

She was a very different kind of person than I was. I had a lot to learn from her. Like a lot of good things, which I've now learned. Not that I'm able necessarily to be like her, but I've learned a whole new concept of consciousness and I didn't know it at the time. I'd go to George and say, "Oh, she drives me nuts, she does that and that and I say blah, blah, blah, and she reacts this way! I can't keep up with it. I just don't know what's happening." So he would support this. He would say, "Well, that's her problem. She's like this. And it's not your fault." So I dug that because it was keeping my head together. But nothing happened, nothing happened.

What I actually learned from Jane is a whole other thing. I could go on for hours. When I first met her I was just like amazed at her ability to move quickly. For her mind to move quickly. Like, if it was a beautiful day, in two minutes she'd know exactly what she wanted to do. No cloudiness in her mind. "I want to do this." We'd get to the park. "Let's go on the boats. Let's sit." Her mind just went so smoothly.

And I was always getting hung up on what people said. You know. *Why did that person say that?* Or hung up on *I didn't do what I was supposed to do.* Everything was so tight, so hung up. I didn't have that freedom, that looseness, that inch of confidence in life that allows you to keep going instead of constantly stopping and say, "Wait a minute. Where am I? What's happening?" You know, to say, "Fuck it. Just keep going. Why do you always have to analyze and think?"

And in fantastic contrast was my therapy, which was forcing me all the time to be aware of what I was doing and why I was doing and what I was thinking and why. And I lost all the pleasure of living. Which wasn't only due to therapy. It was my own thing. My whole childhood was so restricted and regulated. You know, when I was a kid I was really a devil underneath it all. But at home, I was the only child and I was perfect. I did everything right and I said all the right things. So today I'm like very regimented. I always have to say the right thing. I have to be at the right place, clean my house, study, go to work, you know? And do all these things. Go out with a nice clean-cut whatdoyoucallit? American boy, or whatever it is, that my grandmother or my mother would like to imagine me spending time with.

And this person, Jane, she had been through a lot of shit in her childhood. Like her parents had rejected her and she'd been in a reform school. She'd been through so much that she finally sat back one day and looked at it all and said, "Whew, there's nothing I have to bind myself to. Because if life can contain all those absurdities, what's the sense in being attached to anything in particular? Why not just flow with it all. And as long as I'm happy while I'm doing it, what matter does it make to anybody else? It's my life."

And this fantastic amount of freedom just freaked me out.

In our relationship I was very possessive, very neurotic: "I want you to be with me, at this moment. And how dare you go with your friends and leave me behind. You leave me to babysit. You leave me to . . ." you know. And at the time it was all the things that my mother or grandmother would say. Like "How come you didn't bring me home a flower?" All the . . . you know the old biddy biddy wives? That's the way I was. *Nyeh nyeh nyeh nyeh.* "What do you mean? How can you say that? Last week you said blah blah blah and the week before that and I remember when you did this." And she was so free that she'd just look at me and say, "Baby, I can't make that. Good-bye."

Like it was just so alien to her she couldn't even sit down to tell me, "You're driving me nuts with your 'yuptchuptchup tchup tchup.'" She would say instead, "Good-bye. I'll come back some other time." So she'd go. So, "Oh, I'm rejected.

What will I do?" and I was constantly in this bind of, "She just doesn't understand; she's not thoughtful." I'm just saying all kinds of ridiculous nonsense. And she started seeing this other chick and I got very jealous and very up-tight and I wanted to go insane. And so I ended up with this big panic reaction. You know. Shaking and cold and the whole bit.

Yet every time I would get stoned on grass I would notice that I, too, had this freedom. "Oh, you know, I haven't seen Jenny in a long time. I ought to call her up and maybe she'll go to the park with us." And she used to say "Good," And I said, "Wow. I'm doing exactly what she does. And I'm feeling good about it. And I'm not being malicious. Therefore she must not really be being malicious when she does that. She's just feeling what I'm feeling which is raring to go, lots of vitality." So then it came to the point where I said to myself, "Either she's crazy and totally psychotic or I am. But one of us is nuts."

Still I dug that I had to break up with her, because either it was her or me. Or what it was was irrelevant. And I couldn't continue any more with this insane thing that I was going into. So I moved out of the apartment one day in August while she was visiting relatives in New York, and then I became stronger. I got a little hard; it's no big thing, all this nonsense. Which was a brand new feeling for me, and it was like really good. Because she was shot down a little bit because she really dug me.

So she turned around and said, "Now you're a big shit. Now that you've survived something you don't want to see me anymore; meanwhile I still love you." And I still didn't understand this. So I had another step to go. And that was that two people can really dig each other very much and still not want to spend all the time with each other. And still want to have friends and have connections and have things going on, and have their own lives; that is, have their own individual thoughts and feelings about things, and still dig somebody, without constantly mauling each other and this whole sick thing. So that's what I feel I've learned from her.

So anyway, this chick, Jane, and I split up about the time that I first balled George. And as I said, I had sexual problems with men. While I was still in high school I fell in love with a guy and received a great deal of satisfaction from our relationship. Sexually it was very exciting. I didn't climax very often, like maybe twice throughout the whole relationship I had with him, which extended over a period of maybe a year and a half, sporadically. But I knew I was capable of loving a man and digging heterosexual relationships. But he married someone else, and then I didn't climax for about four years, except by masturbation.

And then I met this two-hundred-and-eighty-pound photographer. A very nice person. And I got involved with him. And because of his particular size, weight thing, and the particular position we had sex in, I was able to climax if I had trust and faith in him to let go. We found a position that made it relatively easy for me to climax as long as I could get my head there.* Well, I started to get my head there. So now I know that if I like a guy that I can climax with him.

As a matter of fact, I was seeing this guy at the same time that I was seeing my shrink, George, but the photographer didn't live in my area, so I saw him once a month or something. I straddled on top of him like riding a horse, and his big belly comes up and it rubs against my clit, you see. So while I've got his penis inside me I'm getting clitoral stimulation at the same time which is the easiest way to come. But it's only his big belly that made it so easy. You can do that with any guy but it's a little more difficult, I think.

I never climaxed with a chick. I've not had that much homosexual experience. When I'm with another woman it's

* "Get my head there" refers to Bonnie's being able to psychologically accept this sexual union.

usually a friendly sort of thing, where I dig the person, I'm into her head. Jane, the girl I was living with, was a passive type. She had been a drag butch for years when she was much younger. But that was like years ago. She just wasn't aggressive enough.

I needed more stimulation than this chick was into giving. She said, "If you want a truck driver, then go sleep with a truck driver. But I'm a woman and I'm gentle and I'm soft, and if I can't just squeeze and move a little bit and turn you on, I can't get into anything rough. I can't get in any violent movement because that's not me."

But back to George. He was about forty-three, with a little beard and he kind of dressed sharp, with a leather coat; kind of hip looking for a forty-three-year-old German Jew. Married but separated from his wife for years. And the worst lover in the world.

It had always been disgusting for me when a guy couldn't erect. How do I know that he's up-tight with anybody else? All I know is he's up-tight with me.

And I'd feel like a piece of shit because I'd see him looking at me thinking, "Well, I really got to do this to this woman, because I'm a man. But it's so disgusting."

A person who was more together would say, "Wow, this poor guy has really got a problem." But I used to say, "Oh. I can't take that kind of rejection."

So when George couldn't erect, I just put my head between my hands and I said to myself, "I don't believe this."

I was patient with him but I thought, "Wow! How could he do this to me? He knows—he knew all the time. Months—he knew that anytime I got near a guy who had a little bit of a sexual problem he turned me right off. My whole body was just turned off like a stone.

And his sadism. He says, "You're too nice. You want sex to be loving and affectionate and boo-be-boo-be and cuddling. What's wrong with just erotic physical sex for sex's sake?"

"Nothing," I said. "I've had a lot of sex for sex's sake, maybe even more than you have, considering that you live a very bourgeois kind of life. I've fucked in more places, sometimes with two or three different guys a night, for no money, even. That's not what I'm putting down."

But we didn't have any communication. This was the issue.

And he was so mechanical. I have another lover I climax with and everything is groovy. We fuck underneath the bed, hanging upside down—anyplace. We just have a whole bunch of fun-type things which happen *spontaneously*. But George says, "Okay now. I'm going to get out this table, see, and you're going to put your crotch over here, underneath there, and I'm going to come in from . . ."

So this happened the first time I was with him and it got that way the second time even more so.

He said, "Now look: what's wrong with my saying, 'Put your leg over that table and stand like that now. I'm going to get a stool or something and I'm going to come and put my cock in you this way'?"

What's wrong with it? Ughhh. It's blah. It's not artistically creative. It's just blah, because like I don't dig standing there nude waiting for him to get a stool or to organize his head when I can be fucking upside down, outside, with somebody else, who I'm with.

And he'd pull my hair and spank me. And he would constantly say, "What's wrong with this, doesn't this feel good? It's not pain, it's not pain . . ."

And I would say, "Wow! I don't know if it hurts or not, man, but I'm not having a good time. I just don't dig your pulling my hair right off my head."

And then he'd look intensely at me and bite his lip and he'd growl. That would turn me on in the right instance, but not with him.

But I went back the second time because I wasn't sure of myself and I thought he was right. I thought at the time;

"Wait. Let me get my head together now. He's probably right, because look who he is. And look at me; fucked up sexually. I don't know my identity, blah blah blah. He's a shrink. He must be into something. Maybe it's just my own stupidity."

Because I'd just gone into this thing with Jane, too, realizing that her way of life was like night and day with mine.

And the second time I went back he actually told me "Consider me your teacher."

I felt I don't need any teaching. I just wanted to fuck: "Let's have a sexual thing. I don't want you to teach me anything. If I learn something from you while fucking with you, that's different. But don't go out of your way to put me in a position of . . ."

And then he says, "Well, it's just that you're afraid to be passive."

Which was true. And that's what he kept working on with me.

After the second time I told him, "George, I didn't really know that you had this—you've really got a bit of a hang-up, I think, because regardless of who I am or anything, you should be able to erect if you want to. You should be able to feel your own feelings, regardless of whether I'm Marilyn Monroe or Phyllis Diller, man, or what."

"Oh," he says, "I've been waiting for that. I knew that was coming pretty soon. You're going to start analyzing me and putting down all kinds of things."

Oh, and he got really defensive and really up-tight. So I decided to do something to help him.

I figured this way. If he can't sit there and admit to me that he's got a sexual problem, he's not in contact with himself and there is really no communication between us. Because I was trying to be as open as I could. Because I wanted to be changed. So I made some Alice B. Toklas hashish brownies. And I put five dollars worth of hash in each brownie. And it was a mistake. I'll never do it again. Live and learn.

He doesn't think it was a mistake. He did at first. But after leaving the city's psychiatric ward after a three-day stay he said that he didn't regret the whole thing because he's always wanted to run around downtown in the nude.

There were two things about him I didn't know when I gave him this brownie with hash in it. One is that he's extremely sensitive to drugs, so that when he took this hash (that would make most of us extremely stoned) he was like tripping on heavy, heavy acid. The other thing that I didn't know was that his whole childhood was filled with the Nazis and the running and the killing and the fear. His childhood was paranoia.

And on top of that, since he's content to be a total atheist, he doesn't even have a religious faith to hold on to. So he's afraid of death.

I said, "Let's go for a pack of cigarettes." I thought it would be nice to be outside just when he starts to feel a little stoned. Because he said he had smoked grass before, and he knew what it was like to be stoned. And it's always nice to be in the air and look up, you know? But that was a mistake, to slip drugs on a man who is already paranoid.

So what happened was, because he was allergic to the drug, it came on really quick. I just wanted to go for cigarettes, look at the air. We stopped in a park. And what I didn't know was that he had been mugged twice in that same park; and he knew about a murder there, too.

So he's sitting on a bench, saying, "Oh, what a beautiful sky tonight," and I'm saying, "Yeah, let's go back," when this colored guy walks by with a radio on his ear. And George says to me, "Wait a minute. Why is he walking this way?"

I knew right then that he was getting paranoid. So I said, "Let's go back, George. Let's go back."

On the way back he says, "Wait a minute. I just realized I didn't know where I was in the universe and what time in the history of time it was. I'm totally disoriented. I have no concept of time or distance. What did you give me, acid?" So I said, "No, I gave you some hash."

On the way back he gave all kinds of theories on psychosis and psychology, and he gave me all kinds of theories of consciousness and everything. And if I'd had a tape recorder I could probably make it into a book. He was going on and on, a beautiful rap.

But he kept shifting. "You've infringed upon my things. You know what? I hate you!" He was really crazy, man.

And then we went up the stairs and he mentions his heart, and he says, "I'm going to die. You tell the police you killed me when they come. Will you accept this thing?"

Later when he called up his doctor he was totally insane. He was really freaked out. And I was very up-tight. I couldn't relate to him, I couldn't get to him.

First he went to a neighbor, and he pounded down the door just about, and he went in and he said, "I'm dying, I'm dying." And he walks in the door and while he's dying, in the middle of the whole 'heart attack,' he says, "Oh, what a nice apartment. I never knew that you had such a nice place."

And that's how he kept switching—in and out—from being very aware and very together to being totally freaked out. And then at one point he said to me, "Take off your clothes." He was like snarling about it. And I was trying to get him like back in some way. I didn't want to aggravate him. And I probably dug taking off my clothes, and so I took them off. We were still in this chick's apartment and she didn't even know what was happening.

Then he said, "Now I'm going to do my thing." And he takes off his clothes.

And she's laughing at him because he's telling her how he always wanted to fuck her, because she was sleeping with all these black cats from Africa. She was a professor and she dug the Nigerian students. So his prejudice came out. And she's laughing. And I'm whispering, "Don't laugh . . . don't laugh . . . we're just trying to get together here."

But she kept laughing and he threw a glass of water at her and it smashed all over the fireplace.

Then he gets up and says, "This is a conspiracy. You and she were together and it's a conspiracy against me. The whole thing is a conspiracy."

So then he went back to his apartment and he told the operator to please call his doctor. And he's naked, and he goes back downstairs, and I start chasing him and he runs down the street. And I'm naked and out the front door.

I'm yelling, "George, please, don't go."

I'm pulling at him and he bit my arm (I had to have a tetanus shot). So finally some guys came out and they put a coat over me and they said, "Look, stop trying to chase him because you can't. Look at him. Let him go. There's nothing you can do. Come in and sit."

So I sat down in their apartment and finally he found the police or they found him, or something. They came back. And every once in a while he would look at me, and he would say, "Bonnie, take all these police away. We don't need them. It's okay now." Every once in a while he'd come right through and he'd say, "It's okay. Tell them to go away. I'm all right. I'm all right." And I'd say, "Look. I think he's coming to. It's all right." And the police would say, "Yeah, we know what it's all about." They were so insane. The most insane people in the world.

So we were upstairs and there were seven policemen in the apartment, which wasn't much larger than a closet. And they were harassing him and making fun of him. And I started crying then, because I liked him. Regardless of whatever, I liked him.

I said, "My God, look what I did to him," you know.

And these pigs, I hated their guts. Because they were making fun of him and laughing and they were just being general idiots. So we got dressed, and he's still crazy. In and out—in and out.

So we went to the hospital. And they had cuffed him— hands behind his back. And they marched him in. And by this time he didn't know anything about handcuffs because by this time he was tripping out with the gods.

"I'm still an atheist," he told me later. "But I was doing it. And it was a beautiful experience."

When they took him to the hospital I called some friends out in the country and I said, "Come and get me. Because I can't make this whole ugly scene."

I stayed in the country a couple of days. Then I came back and saw George at the hospital. He was completely recovered. He had recovered almost immediately, but he was staying in the hospital to rest up.

Then I started to see another psychiatrist, Gerald, the same guy that my girl friend had been going to for five years— whom she'd slept with. And I told him, "I really don't want to go back to George. Because he turns me off."

But I didn't know what else to say. Because now the guy is writing me letters and he's hung up and it was really starting to get very icky. Like he'd send me flowers and write poetry about cocks and things. And he was very crazy. His entire reality was symbolic. Even sexual movements were done as a symbol of something else. And in his room he must have had four or five hundred sun symbols. In the form of a pot holder, a painting, a sculpture. Everything in his room.

So Gerald said, "Don't. Don't go back."

And then I got a telegram from George that really ended it. It said something about meeting him at nine o'clock that night in his bed. And it went on to say, "If you don't come, if you're not there, then you don't deserve to get the man that I am." And really, I just couldn't relate to that, because he was like telling me, "If you don't want to fuck with me, if you don't come up here . . . you're not a woman."

Well, this really shot me down, because even though we'd gone through all of these hassles, I still respected him as a man, I respected him as a person, and I relied on his acceptance of me a great deal—and this hurt. I had felt that I could go to him and tell him anything. I could tell him that I killed somebody, I could tell him that I masturbate, and how and why and where, and it wouldn't make any difference to him. So the knowledge that I could do that made me think, "Wow, what an intimacy we have! It's so beautiful." And then he turns around and this man, that I've vested all this interest in and all this security and trust all this time turns around and tells me, "You're not a woman." It really shot me down.

I just sat there and cried.

He had given me the keys to his apartment because I was painting it for seventy dollars (I needed the bread). So instead of going up as he had instructed, I just left the keys in his mailbox. Because the moment I'd read, "If you don't come . . ." I said to myself, "Uh, uh. Ain't no way that he can make me."

So he sent me a letter, saying, "You really hurt me. When I came home and found the keys in the box and you were not there it shot me down and blah blah blah . . ."

So I wrote him a letter and I said, "I don't want to hear about it anymore. Because how you could have the insensitivity with my sexual problems to tell me that I'm not a woman, just because I don't want to sleep with you maybe, is too much and blah blah blah."

So then he wrote me back saying, "I apologize. You're right. I've been hostile because you didn't stay overnight that night, but as I was hostile to you I also have a bit of love for you on the other side. So don't take all of my aggressions, all of my hostilities, and call it me. Remember there are many sides of me."

So I thought, "Okay, groovy. Out of sight. But I'm finished with this game. I can't be involved with it anymore because it's not getting me anywhere, it's not helping me. I'm uptight." It made me nauseous to go see him. And my shrink said not to. I didn't let George know that I had a new shrink because I felt that really would be too much for him. That would really be nasty.

So then I got into yoga and acid. And the combination of those two things and a couple of experiences of being on acid with some of the high yogi's made me . . . I don't know . . . but one day, about five or six months ago, I woke up.

And for the first time in my life, I looked around and I said, "Wow, I'm here." And my roommate, Jane, was there too, and I looked at her and I said, "You've been here all the time? Why didn't you tell me?"

And she says, "You go out tomorrow and try to tell somebody that's not here about here. There's no way that you can conceive of hereness until they experience it. You can talk and talk and write books, you can do anything. And the only thing that will get them here is maybe singing them a song, letting them meditate, or whatever."

Now I'd taken acid several times, but I had never gotten into the yoga thing in addition to it. So then I just started to get myself together much more after that.

I haven't seen George. I went to see Gerald to get over the guilt about George being in the psychiatric ward for three days because of the stuff I gave him. But I overcame the guilt almost immediately when he came around and told me he'd had a good time running around downtown in the nude and had always wanted to trip out. He said, "The only thing I'm a little bit upset about is I'm getting kicked out of the apartment, possibly for the same ruckus."

So the guilt thing was over, but I still went to see Gerald because my friends said I should. (Today, either I do something because I want to do it, or I don't do it. I'm more into my own thing now.)

And I kept telling Gerald, I said, "When I first started therapy a year and a half ago with George, after the session, especially before I went to the Caribbean, he would get into such nitty-gritty things I would be in pain all week. But I felt like I was participating in a process of some kind. With you I come, I sit, and nothing happens. When I leave you, nothing's happening. I'm not at all involved in this."

He says, "What do you want me to do? You want me to make you cry next week?"

I said, "Yeah. Sure. Why not. Something's got to happen. Because I'm getting bored. I'm really being fucking bored, getting tired of telling you what I did last week when I really don't give a shit what I did last week. Which is my thing, maybe. Maybe we just don't go together, as therapist and patient."

Finally he said to me: "I don't think that you should come anymore because you're not suffering. I don't know what I'm treating you for. You seem not to have any anxiety or what not and I don't know what I'm seeing you for." So then I went directly into yoga. And that's what I've been into now.

In spite of all the things that I went through with George, I think George is a good therapist, within the context of psychoanalysis. I don't think Gerald did anything for me because I think psychoanalysis is limited to a particular state of mind and particular kind of people. And I just wasn't in that state of mind to relate to it then. I think Gerald was good. I think they were both very good. But maybe Gerald was a little more together.

The sexual experience with George was painful in many ways. And when I finally came to the point when I learned there are really groovy men in this world—good people that happen to have a penis—sincere, gentle, affectionate people, that was a great discovery. Because the only person I knew like that was my grandfather. But he was also very castrated because of my grandmother.

All of a sudden I met the photographer who was sincerely interested in me and said, "Look. I want to make you satisfied. And I don't care what it does to my ego or what. I like you, I believe in you. I respect you. I love you in a certain way." And he meant it. He was a beautiful person. Because he was concerned about me. He dug me. And I said, "Wow. There are really people like that."

But to my shrink, if I would go by what happened between him and me to make a judgment about men, phew! I'd really be in pretty bad shape. Even if he had been into S and M and together with it, I probably would have said, "Wow, I've never had the experience with S and M things. What better way to get into it than with a man that I trust." Why not? I'm not afraid of getting into S and M. I'm not afraid of getting into any particular thing. But it was his up-tightness, his sexual inabilities that made it impossible to get into the little things with him, let alone something experimental like that.

I'm glad that it worked out the way it did. Because as I look back on it, I wouldn't want to have had a relationship with a therapist. Because I think it's kind of sick, for a chick with sexual problems to be having an occasional affair-type relationship with this middle-aged man who has his own sexual problems—a guy who like every New Year's Eve goes out with the same chick, who happens to be a butch lesbian.

If I had it to do all over again, I'd do it the same way, because if it took whatever it took for me to come where I am now, I'm happy.

I think I could have had better experiences—more valuable experiences. I don't think I learned anything significant, outstandingly significant by sleeping with George.

The same thing is true of my friend who slept with Gerald. She said, "I learned that he was a human being. That he came and he was basic and all those things. I learned that, and it was no big thing. And I lost the God image of him."

Maybe that's one thing it does. If you think somebody is God it certainly brings that all down. And I had thought that he was very perceptive, very aware. I thought that he was understanding. Which he was in the context of psychoanalysis.

So I'm glad I did it and I'm glad I got out. For me to be continuing with George would have been just wallowing in neurosis instead of jumping out of it. I did get into an encounter group recently because that's so closely related to what I'm into now—sensory awareness. And the whole orientation is exactly what I feel now—a continuum of experiences. To touch and smell a flower is a continuum of a great yogi cat sitting there meditating on his seventh shakra. I think it's all on the same continuum—just a different part of the same progression.

I think that occasionally fucking with a therapist is essentially no different from sitting there rapping to him. I don't see what the big thing is, sleeping with your therapist. But I think that, unfortunately, too much of the time not only is the patient's motivation fucked up but the therapist's motivation is fucked up. Where a therapist is capable of having a very accurate outlook on the whole situation and on himself—where he understands himself—I don't think it's any big thing. I mean especially in a one-to-one relationship where you've been going to somebody for a while. You've been seeing him, you dig him, you rely on him, and you trust him. What's wrong with having a sexual thing with him? I don't think there's anything inherently wrong with that.

AUTHOR'S POSTSCRIPT

In essence, this relationship is one in which the therapist is a lot sicker than Bonnie. But ironically, she discovered her strength in comparison to his weakness, even though the exposure of his weakness doomed the therapy. Starting on a one-to-one therapist-patient basis, the relationship exploded into a kind of encounter. Though Bonnie talks about her disgust, she also ended up with a certain sympathy for George as a human being, and a respect for him as a therapist. George seems to have destroyed a potentially useful therapeutic situation because of his inability to act therapeutically while sexually involved.

Bonnie is someone who would never have been likely to hold intimacy against George had it not been extraordinarily inept and ill-advised. I think that this case throws into strong relief the fact that intimacy, even when permissible, sought after, and reliably undestructive from the patient's point of view, must be carefully weighed and abandoned if the therapist's interests and functional abilities go counter to the patient's strivings. As Bonnie said, in view of George's knowledge of her attitudes toward impotence, his offer of intimacy was extremely antitherapeutic.

It also seems clear that her experiences with Jane, with drugs, and with her photographer friend were profoundly more growth-producing (and therapeutic) than any of her contacts in formal psychotherapy. Psychotherapists in particular should be aware of the limitations of formal systems of therapy, in contrast to the rich and varied informal influencing systems in some of our patients' lives.

And finally, as we have seen previously, the therapist, too, can run great personal hazards through intimate involvement with his patient.

12

NICHOLAS

"It was the greatest experience of my life"

*A former high-level employee of the Federal govern-
ment, currently between jobs, Nicholas makes one think of
the proverbial book clerk. Although only thirty-nine, he looks
years older. Short and slight, with thinning, reddish hair and a
long, thin moustache, and wearing a nondescript business suit
and tie, he carries himself in a way that would indicate pas-
sivity and shyness. When we meet he is somewhat suspicious
about my credentials but I am able to put his doubts to rest
with relative ease.*

At age nineteen I was aware that I needed help and sought
it out on my own with very little support from my family. At
the time I was in a real deep depression, which, no matter
what I did, I couldn't shake. I went to an internist who happened to be treating some other members of my family and he
recommended that I go see a psychiatrist. And it was a real
bad scene. I was very poor at the time and couldn't afford it.
So I went about four times and it was very stressful and I
couldn't afford it and he suggested the mental-hygine clinic.
So I went down and signed up shortly afterward and there
was about a six-month wait.

During that period it was the funniest thing. I was very

religious at the time. I related it to a novena I had made at St. Patrick's: that in November the clouds started breaking and I started coming out of it a bit, and in December I started going to the city hospital's psychiatric out-patient clinic. And just prior to going, I'd also fallen in love with my wife-to-be, which was the first real feelings of love I've had for anybody. So by the time I got to the clinic, as the lady psychiatrist I was assigned to said, I had in many respects pulled myself up by my bootstraps. Having had one semester of psychology, I refer to it as my spontaneous recovery.

I was doing a hell of a lot better when I got to her and I probably stayed with her for about eighteen months—about nine months before I got married and about nine months afterward. And I think that that experience as a psychiatric experience and a helping experience was useful to me, although I decided I'd gotten a good deal on my own. So I terminated this, and it wasn't until about four or five months after the death of my wife, which was in nineteen fifty-eight, that I felt the need for psychiatry again.

I had moved in with my brother and his wife and I was making an adjustment to the death of my wife very well, and then my brother asked me to find new quarters. The only other choice I had was to go back with my mother. And this led me back almost to the identical feelings I had at age nineteen. I needed some way to get out of the place I was in or else there was no point in life.

I had told a few people what I was experiencing, and one of the girls at work said that they had a group going at work. (I worked on some important government projects and this is why I asked for your credentials). I made contact with the psychiatrist there, on the staff, told him my problem and also suggested that I get clearance to go back to the clinic, but he suggested going to this group. And that was very helpful. Within about six weeks I was able to grab hold of what had put me into this depression, which was the adjustment back to the mother situation, after all these years of being away to find myself a little boy again. And I terminated there nine months after adjusting to the situation.

It was kind of painful for my mother for a period of time thereafter, my resurgence as a human being. As I told Ralph (the psychiatrist I eventually became intimate with) at one time, it was a goddamn good experience to continue living there and to sort of train my mother—not train her, but for the two of us to find each other as adults rather than as parent and child. I still, financially and more than financially, needed her support because my kids were very small, and she could help with them.

Then, four or five years later, I found myself getting back in this frame of mind, this not wanting to be with anybody, this complete withdrawal. And so I went back again to a psychiatrist. And I found out at that time that what I was dealing with was a fellow that I had brought in as my assistant, who was about four years younger than I was. And I found myself in this younger brother thing that I had dealt with throughout my life in terms of my father. And I got myself into a bind because I was working for a man whom I liked very much and who respected me very much. But this boss looked upon the younger fellow as the guy who could sort of fix his automobile and do all these boy/man things which I always felt inadequate in. And I felt I was really being totally nosed out.

So anyway, I was able to, after another period of six or eight weeks, grab hold of this. And then, back in nineteen sixty-five, I was asked to do some work in Asia. And it was a long span between the time they asked me and the time they needed me over there. And after the initial excitement abated, I started getting concerned over how my kids were going to adjust, just the four of us going—without my mother to take care of them. And so I did something indirectly, which got me off the hook from transferring to Asia.

Way back when I went for my draft physical, I surfaced my homosexual tendencies. In nineteen fifty-seven, when my wife was still alive, I was given a delicate overseas assignment that required me getting a top-level security clearance. And part of that clearance involved the government's getting in touch with my draft board, which in turn immediately told my superiors, "Look. You've got a homosexual on your hands." So there was a big to-do and they brought me in for a polygraph. And this canceled out that mission. Shortly after that I was given a different assignment. This didn't seem to upset the department's people except for the fact that they had to polygraph me.

When I was given the polygraph, I told them exactly what happened when I went through my army physical. I checked the box, that said, "Do you have homosexual tendencies?" And then I talked to a psychiatrist. And that was just about three or four months before I first went to the hospital's outpatient clinic, and after I had started working for the department. So none of that had ever come out in my initial processing for the department. But in nineteen fifty-seven they brought it up in my polygraph, so they knew.

I didn't know that every adult man or boy had this at some time, so it loomed very large in my thinking, my anxiety and concern about homosexual tendencies, my erotic response to males. It was merely psychosexual. It was in my head and in my feelings. I guess that at age nineteen, when I got this first real depression, I wasn't sure which sex I was. And in the depression I used to categorize myself as sort of a neuter. Because I guess by that time I found myself so fucked up in these feelings of guilt, that I was having these longings. And even though these were only fantasies, I had not clarified within my own mind that having these thoughts was all right. And I remained tortured by these thoughts, even through my marriage.

I had a real good experience when this first came out in

nineteen fifty-seven. This was a great feeling, to know that I had carried this great burden all these years and to know that it wasn't all that destructive to my career. I guess maybe then I was beginning to hear, but not beginning to believe, that most people have these kinds of feelings to a greater or lesser degree.

So it was great. And I guess in many respects it lessened the anxiety tremendously, and with respect to my relationship with my wife this made me feel, "Well, you're really normal after all." And during that period it was the best two years of my marriage, relationshipwise and sexualwise. But I still had these anxieties about this homosexual feeling, and about six months later I really settled back again, with respect to these anxieties and feeling that I'm not normal and, you know, buying beefcake magazines and that sort of thing. Something which I developed and had guilt feelings about.

Then I went on a temporary assignment for about six weeks down in the Far East. I had a pretty lonely time and a lot of anxieties over masturbation. I felt it was wrong and dirty and childish and showed lack of self-control. And the first night I was back with my wife I went to bed with her and this was the first night I couldn't get a hard-on. And that was just devastating. It was so surprising and devastating to her that she laughed.

I came back from abroad in November or December. And I guess she got pregnant just before I went down there. She died the following year, and I've told you how I felt after that about my brother and mother.

Anyway, that's history to explain what I did back in nineteen sixty-five. Rather than go directly and tell my superiors that I didn't want to go to Asia because I had some feelings of insecurity and I had built up a lot of my own resources here in the States and didn't really want to give them up, I went and said, "Look, this happened back in nineteen fifty-seven and it might happen again if I go back on another assignment which requires another security clearance." This was a real concern, but you know it was a real double kind of deal.

And then shortly after that I remember going to a Christmas party and this gal showing me a picture, I guess of her daughter and her son-in-law. They were both in bathing suits. And this guy really turned me on. I couldn't give a damn about the daughter. This really got to me, particularly with the job being canceled and not quite knowing what was going to happen. So I said to myself, "Goddamn. You're going to have to deal with this." And this concern and anxiety always seem to become prominent when I have other things not going well in my life.

So I went back to the shrink at work. This was in sixty-six. And I brought a lot of this up in our group analysis. I said, "Look. I want to deal with this for once and for all." And I said, "I still don't have the money to see a private therapist and so I want to go back to one of the clinics in the city." But he didn't want me to do that. He said, "What I'd like you to do is talk with a psychoanalyst. I think psychoanalysis is in order. You talk to him. They do have a program where they have a reduced fee, something or other, and maybe you can work out something there."

So this psychoanalyst came in as a consultant (he had been an employee of the department) and we had two hour-and-a-half interviews. And he said, "You need psychoanalysis. You're a homosexual."

So he put me in touch with this other guy in private practice, and I went down and talked to him and told my story. And he said, "Yeah. You need it."

He was one of the guys that was supposed to be in this program of reduced time or, really, reduced fee for time spent. And he said he didn't have any time then but that he would get in touch with me when he did. I guess he never did. I got in touch with him once or twice and he said, "No, I still don't have any time."

So time went on and things sort of settled back to normal again. And then I saw my opportunity to go into therapy outside of a clinic situation, because I had a windfall of some money. A relative died and willed me enough money that I thought I could get started—what with the insurance paying fifty per cent at the time.

At that time I was going with a gal who had just finished with a well-known psychoanalyst. She was going to him and thought he was the greatest and said, "Even if he doesn't have any free time he could see you and refer you to somebody." I went to see him and talked to him and liked him very much. He didn't have any free time but he said, "I'll give you the names of some other analysts that I think will be able to be helpful to you." And one of them was Ralph.

I almost didn't get to go to Ralph because he said he didn't have any openings at that time, but he would call me back in the next couple of weeks and let me know. Ralph didn't call me and I called him again and I was quite angry and he did make an appointment for me.

We started off, I guess, just once a week for the first few times. I decided I liked him and he liked me and he would take me on. So then we met more frequently.

It was the greatest experience in my life, at least one of the greatest experiences, experiencing Ralph.

After we got over the preliminaries, he said, "I have only two rules. One is that you let me know your feelings toward me at the moment they happen. This is how I work with patients and this is what I'm most interested in. And the other is that pay day is the first of the month." And I got a little fouled up with that because I took him literally and he kind of clarified this later. For on occasion I would go down very upset or depressed about something in my life and rather than bring this out, I just kept it there because of what he said. But anyway that only happened a couple of times.

We got right down to business about what my concern was.

We started off rather slowly, and then I remember after about six weeks again that we were talking about my homosexual feelings. And he said, "You know, you turn me on."

This came as a surprise and just a real good feeling, that somebody else, another married man, is willing to admit this, and "Goddamn, this is good."

I remember telling him all my concerns in this area, and he said, "Have you ever slept with a man?" And I said "No," and his response was, "That's too bad."

So anyway, I guess it was a few sessions after that that he told me about his responses toward me, and I thought, "Well there's nothing really wrong with you after all."

I was very relieved, sort of like the last line in *Portnoy's Complaint*, "Now we can begin." And so we did. I guess I was about six or eight weeks into therapy.

During this time, too, he had told me on a number of occasions about his relationship with some of his men friends and the intimacy thereof. At that point I had a fear even of a man touching me beyond shaking his hand. And he told me about hugging men and embracing them. I don't know if at this point he told about going to bed with men. Anyway, he indicated enough to me to get me thinking about the fact that this wasn't all bad. At one point I had told him that I had thought about wanting to put my hand on his leg.

And he said, "Is that all you wanted to do?"

And I said, "That's all I permitted myself to think about."

And he said, "Well, open up your mind and see where you'd really like your hand to go."

At this time he was going to take a week or so off, And I had started to let my mind open up and see just where my hand wanted to go. First my hand wanted to go up in his crotch and all over his body. And I had just a fantastic experience while he was away that he entitled "imaginative reality," where I actually lived with him in all kinds of sexual situations. Just lived in a state of what I called ecstatic euphoria, being totally turned on. I was just sort of floating on the ceiling and having dry orgasms. Just all kinds of fantastic feelings going through my body. And all this was happening while he was away.

When he came back I was ready to just drag him into bed, but he wasn't ready for it. As a matter of fact, he told me that the way I was acting kind of disgusted him; I was trying to seduce him and whatnot. This threw me into a fantastic state of rejection. And the feelings themselves were just as intense. I did a lot of crying and screaming and what not, mainly by myself.

I just felt miserable, and felt like a tramp and felt like any number of other awful things. And this sort of all settled down after a couple of more sessions. Then we continued to talk about my fear of intimacy with another man, and also my desire for intimacy with another man. And he continued to relate some stories of his own experiences. And I guess it was shortly after that period where I had worked myself up into this euphoria that he told me that he wasn't available to me in this kind of relationship and, you know, "Go find your own."

Just before going to him I had broken up with this girl who referred me to the analyst who sent me to Ralph. So I was sort of companionless for this period of time. I started in December and it wasn't until March that I found another gal friend. And in a sense she sort of helped to take the pressure off my desire to have Ralph as a sexual partner.

I remember at one point a hassle where I got quite angry with him and said, "Goddamn it. You sit over there and talk about all these other relationships, and you say this is a possibility with us. Shit or get off the pot."

And I guess that's when he first came over to the couch— and I got quite frightened. He put his arm around me. And I sort of condemned it a little bit. Then we laid down for a little while and hugged. We were fully clothed. That was kind of nice, although I still had all kinds of fears. And I sort of kept my cock away from touching any part of his body. He called my attention to that. I wasn't totally responsive. And we sort of worked through this.

The next time or so we again became quite intimate touching each other, still fully clothed. And I guess it was shortly after that that we were lying and embracing and we were very passionate with each other. And I slipped his pants off, stuck his cock in my mouth, blew him, and it was just a fantastic scene. After that, part of the sessions sooner or later became sexual encounters.

This intimacy began about six months after I began seeing him. Within another four months I felt ready to leave. He felt that there were some other areas that we might work on. So I stayed on an additional four months before terminating with him.

Most of the time I was seeing him three times a week and we would have sexual encounters or simply hugs nearly every session after it began. We would quite often post-mortem our sexual experience in terms of my response and his response; whether or not we felt we were really into each other in terms of being with each other or if we were this place or that place or if we were conning each other or whatever.

In many respects he was being the teacher or instructor. Not in terms of technique, but in terms of discussing feelings that were occurring in an embrace maybe, without anything beyond that.

This memory always stands out particularly in terms of his technique:

I popped into his office one morning and I said something that he didn't pick up. I guess he didn't hear me, all the words that I was saying. I expected him to laugh because it was something that occurred in the prior session, but he didn't, so I was angry. But this was obscured, and I started to talk about something that was going on outside our relationship, and was talking quite rapidly about it. All of a sudden I stopped and heaved a sigh, and he said, "Stop right there. Now what's that all about?"

I didn't know at the time what it was all about. But we spent about half an hour tracing back what had happened to make me cover again this story I had been telling, what my real feeling was, which was a feeling of hurt. So we finally got back to that second at the door when I made the remark and he didn't respond. And he explained that I had brought up some history that he hadn't immediately recognized.

So while we stopped in February of sixty-nine it wasn't the end of the story at all. The day I left—it's funny, the day I was supposed to leave he cut his nose. He was doing some jogging in the morning and I had pulled up in front of his house just as he was coming across the yard with all this blood running down his face. So he went inside and I went inside and he was in the back there and he finally came out and he said, "Look. My wife has to take me to the hospital so I can't see you this morning." And he made another appointment the following week. I sort of regarded this as his Freudian "slip," because he didn't really want me to go.

So at the last session I said to him, "Am I ever going to see you again?" and he said, "It's partly up to you and it's partly up to me." And so I decided, "This is the end, I'm going to deal with it."

From the point of view of intimacy the only other relationship that was as intimate was the one with my wife. And that isn't an easy kind of thing to break off.

Yet I was doing okay. A number of times I wanted to go back and see him again but I decided, "You're finished now, work with it."

I was doing okay until I decided to give up cigarettes, and got myself into a group for that purpose. I had been a heavy smoker for twenty years, and I went into a real state of depression. I can't imagine anyone cutting off narcotics as having suffered more than I did. I just cried at the least little thing that happened to me. This persisted for maybe three or four weeks after I started the program. Finally I just decided I couldn't go any longer with that scene, and so I called Ralph up and told him I wanted to go back and see him.

I did and I told him the whole story of giving up the cigarettes and how I'd been suffering. He was quite angry that I had not gotten in touch with him before. And I was angry that he didn't tell me in February that there was this possibility. I maybe also feel that we should have tapered off a little more gradually.

But prior to doing any talking we immediately went to bed. And I was fantastically passionate.

I remember his looking up at me and saying, "Did you say you had a problem?"

So, anyway, we discussed this cigarette thing. It was real good to be with him again.

I saw him three or four times after that. We got very much involved sexually, to a point where that was all that was going on. He was concerned about this because he suggested bringing in somebody else, a woman.

He said, "I think you need a woman. I know this gal therapist and I'd like to bring her down and have the three of us sit together and try to work this out." What he meant was to work out the sexual relationship in terms of my breaking it off again and his feeling that he wasn't totally able to do it by himself.

He was saying, "Look. All we're doing now is going to bed with each other. I think we ought to have someone a little more objective work with us to put this back into focus."

To the best of my memory that's what it was all about. I felt it was a matter of he may have bitten off more than he could chew. I guess the two of us discussed the fact that this was someplace where we didn't always want to be. We both felt that it needed looking at—he more than I, actually.

So he brought this gal in. I thought it was going to be somebody I didn't know. I knew this woman analyst, which wouldn't have made any difference except that I couldn't stand her. And when I walked in the door, there she was sitting. I think I picked up all kinds of hostile and negative feelings immediately, but stuffed them all back. And we had a real good session together, he and I. I forgot what exactly went on but I remember during the whole session we sat opposite each other. Then all three of us planned to meet again. And in the interim I went through the same kind of experience that I described—this "imaginative reality" thing—with her. Except that I was killing her in a number of ways and with total feeling.

So I went back to the second session and sort of relived a lot of these feelings of hostility and anger and hate and desire to kill, with her. And it got Ralph very upset and he thought I was acting very childish and immature.

After the session was over she asked, "Do you want us to meet again?" and I said, "Never again."

And he said, "Listen. I've got a big investment in the relationship and I don't mean moneywise."

He meant that which existed between the two of us. I forget exactly what he said, but he didn't want to see me run off, or whatever. But he wasn't going to see me again unless I saw him with her. So I said, "I'll let you know."

I gave several days of thought to this and called him up and said, "I can't and I won't do it. I'm sorry that it had to work out this way, and I'd very much like to see you." So I said, "So long," and he said, "Wait a minute, You know I make mistakes too." And so we kicked that around a bit and he said, "I think what might be useful for the two of us would be for you to come to my group in August." This was in June or July. And so I said "Okay, I'd like to do that."

Ralph was doing group work with a cotherapist, Earl, at

that time (when I joined the group) and, God, that was a painful thing because Ralph had such an intimate friendship with Earl. But I was able to see them together and able to accept that. We had a couple of exercises together, the three of us. It was a weekend group and we finally got around to work some things out in the relationship. And by the time the weekend finished and time went on I felt that I could feel my way through this.

Then, in September or October, Ralph called me at work one day and said, "I want to see you. Meet me for lunch." So I said, "Sure."

I was real excited and I wasn't sure what it was all about, but it was always exciting for me to be with him. So we met at a restaurant, and, God, was he in a bad way! I'd never seen him so out of it.

He told me he was living with feelings of rejection from Earl. And he turned to me. I couldn't feel any greater; his seeking me out for this kind of reason. So we had lunch together, and then went over to his home, went to bed together, and later Earl came back. Ralph was feeling much better when I left that evening.

Needless to say, I was elated at having been called by him in this way. But then several days later I got very disconsolate and angry and I called him up and told him that it just wasn't fair. I had gone to the group in August, and I was beginning to work out my dependency on him. I was beginning to . . . I had done a good job. I was moving forward in other directions and it just wasn't fair for him to pull me back.

He said, "Yeah. You're right. But there are a lot of things in life that aren't fair." So I remember at the end of the conversation he said, "Hey. I love you very much." And that sort of made things very right again.

Of course after that, after his making me aware of the fact that he saw me at least in this instance as an important person, I wanted him again. I wanted to be with him again and go to bed with him.

And I called him a couple of weeks thereafter, sort of in a maudlin, weepy, whiny, crying mood. I had been drinking and working on it. And he said, "If you get off this whiny crap, I'd like to have you come down." So I got off the whiny crap and went down. His whole family was on vacation at the time, and Earl was living there at the house.

We went out that evening and had something to eat and came back and spent the night together. That was the first time, the first and only time, that I spent the night with him.

Then I guess I didn't see him for a while. I may have had one or two appointments in the winter. And then last February, I made the decision to retire from my job. I had manipulated the situation so that I could have my job abolished and get termination pay and whatnot, and I did it. I was beginning to get a little anxious about what I had done. So I called him up and went to see him. We kicked this around for a while, and then we went to bed again—spent much more time together than the therapeutic hour. And then time went on . . .

I called him one night about a month ago and he suggested meeting for lunch. We did about two weeks later, and that's when he brought up this business of your wanting to talk to people like me. And then he said, "I do want to see you sometime, not as your therapist, but there have been so many demands on my time, that I haven't really been able to give time to anybody except my children and family.

This to me was very real. He was very honest about it. The last time I saw him was last week when I called him and said I wanted to come down and see him therapeutically; that I was hung up about this job searching. So I went down and saw him and it wasn't a very good scene—not that it was a bad one.

The best thing about seeing Ralph was getting over this

fear of intimacy with men. The fear of being touched by men or touching a man; just touching—not fucking. That has been the greatest thing, and along with that the ability to express affection to another man. And feeling this from him and allowing him the freedom to let this happen.

The worst thing is the continuing relationship in terms of my still wanting him more than he's available to me. But the good tremendously outweighs the pain.

With men I now have tremendous amounts of freedom. Since Ralph I've not been sexually intimate with any man, but not through any fault of my own. Right now I'm living through, I don't know how to phrase it, a distorted over-emphasis of my own on my homosexuality, to the exclusion of almost everything else. I don't like this. I don't dislike it, but I would like to have what I would consider to be a little more balanced sexual thinking and responding. But I think of this as a temporary thing, and it will abate.

There's this one fellow I met at a marathon a couple of months ago and I see him occasionally. The freedom that the two of us have together about expressing affection, about expressing homosexuality, is something I've never had before in my life. This guy, he's a funny guy in that he's very affectionate physically. We will hug and kiss on occasion, that sort of thing, but this is where he says he stops in terms of any relationship with a man. So this I feel is a real fantastic gain in my coping with my feelings. There aren't any other men in my life where I have the freedom I have with this guy, but I feel that my openness invites at least a little more honesty on the part of another male in terms of his feelings toward me.

The other therapists I saw never helped me come to grips with what ailed me, not the way Ralph did. In these two group things at work we just kind of touched on it. It was always a crisis situation, and once having gotten over the crisis I would terminate.

AUTHOR'S POSTSCRIPT

Before commenting on this case I find it necessary to state that I do not consider homosexuality an illness to be cured of. A homosexual impulse exists in all of us. So do heterosexual impulses. The so-called "fag queen" who is incapable of recognizing and accepting his heterosexual feelings is as blind as the Don Juan who cannot get in touch with the homosexual side of his nature.

Given this range of sexual desires, every man and woman must find his own resting point on the homo-heterosexual axis.

This was apparently something Nicholas could not do. Before meeting Ralph he was both plagued by, and ashamed of, his strong homosexual impulses. They yearned for fulfillment, yet caused much guilt. Ralph both helped the flower bloom and removed the shame by encouraging a homosexual liaison within the therapeutic framework.

Ralph's fantastically direct, if unorthodox, way helped Nicholas solve this particular problem. It has been my observation that patients with similar problems usually go on for years in therapy without resolving the issue. In fact, Nicholas did just that before meeting Ralph.

The only flaw I see in an otherwise totally positive therapeutic situation was caused by Ralph's failure to pay enough attention to Nicholas's dependency. Ralph performed admirably when Nicholas returned to treatment by bringing in a female consultant. Bringing in this "outsider" scotched Nicholas's tendency to tie himself to Ralph in a binding way. And Ralph re-emphasized his role as a therapist, as opposed to being a lover.

On the other hand, Ralph's negligence in this regard was clear when he called upon Nicholas for comfort and sex when Ralph's family was away and Earl was rebuffing him. Ralph's own neediness interfered with his concern for his patient. It was not that Nicholas wanted out of homosexuality as much as he needed to find a sexual relationship that was capable of providing greater intimacy than the one he had with Ralph.

He needed a *primary* relationship, not a secondary one. And Ralph already had a wife and a male lover. For Nicholas, such unrequited love could only lead to additional frustrations.

Nonetheless, if therapists are supposed to be catalysts for change and growth, I can think of few instances of therapy as useful and dramatic as this one.

13

GERALD AND MONICA

"Conventional society would freak out about this"

This account is presented in the original interview form because I wished to distinguish the statements made by each of the two subjects. I talked with Gerald and Monica in their attractive, small apartment, simply yet quite distinctively furnished. In some ways it seemed to reflect Gerald's foreign birth and his interest in law, which he teaches at a large Eastern university.

Gerald's bearing is gentle and polite. Over six feet tall, thirty years old, blond, slim, and upright, he looks somewhat like a Prussian Jean Pierre Aumont.

His wife, Monica, in contrast to Gerald's freshly starched appearance, is clad in a loose-fitting burlap sack dress. She is twenty-seven, wears no make-up or jewelry. Dark-haired and cherubic looking, she is slightly pudgy though inviting. One would never guess that she is a former model, actress, and playwright.

Many small, sincere, taken-for-granted affectionate gestures were periodically exchanged between the two without ostentation.

Shepard: I'd like you to tell me as freely as you can about how you came to see the therapists you were intimately in-

*volved with, what your history of involvement with therapists
is in general, what you went into treatment for in the first
place, what you got out of treatment with these people (as
compared to other therapists you saw), and what role sexual
intimacy played in whatever you got from them.*

Gerald: To start with, my very first experience with a therapist was in Europe when I was very down over a crisis in
my Ph.D. studies. I simply wanted to use the school psychologist to help me get out of my down, and to sort of help myself
reaffirm myself and to get going again. So I saw this man for
about five or six weeks and it worked. As soon as I was finished I said, "Thank you very much. That was very good of
you. I'm fine now. I don't want to see you anymore." My
attitude toward psychiatrists and psychologists in general was
that crazy people went to see them, and I was embarrassed
about having been thrust into a position where I felt it was
necessary to see one.

The next experience was after we had gotten married,
which was a very quick decision. We hadn't seen each other in
five years, and we suddenly decided to get married, and in the
five years when we hadn't seen each other we developed
rather diverging paths of thinking, attitudes, and all sorts of
things. But on the other hand, we had also grown up. We'd
become much more open and much more communicative.

Yet about four or five or six months later we developed
some of these tensions. We suddenly started finding fault with
each other, and we no longer were as concerned with supress-
ing finding fault, for reasons of not wanting to hurt the other
person's feelings. Some severe tensions developed over this
because I was constantly suggesting ways in which Monica
ought to do things differently in the kitchen and household,
and was critical of her cleanliness and also little things, you
know. And we grew apart, and it reached sort of a climax at a
party one evening when we just barely looked at each other

and mostly growled. A friend of ours at that stage suggested that we go see Larry.

At first I was pretty hostile toward the idea, but then on the other hand I thought, "Well, I must be open about this." And later on I decided, "Well, maybe it isn't such a bad idea after all." I was in the navy at the time, incidentally, and Larry was a psychiatrist, with the community mental health board, and I could just drive up from work (or take a taxi from work) and go see him at his office. It was just a few blocks and we'd have some time to talk things over.

At first it was pretty stilted, pretty stiff. Because this was all, again, a relatively strange experience for me. And I was sort of doing this on the understanding of, "Well, I'll do it just to see what—if anything—might come of this that might help me." It wasn't until Larry shifted the venue to his house that the meetings became much more relaxed and we became more intimate.

And I remember distinctly the first time Larry said, "Let's take off our clothes."

And I said, "Oh God, what are we getting into?"

But we took off our clothes. I took off everything except my shorts at that time, and Larry didn't push me. And then we talked about my fear of latent homosexuality—two men being undressed together and things like that.

Monica at this time simply knew that I was seeing Larry, knew and encouraged me. I suppose we talked, afterward at home, about what was happening. At any rate, at another time we again took off all our clothes and we hugged, Larry's object being to get me over this body fear and this fear of being afraid of other male contact. This was a very strong thing with me. I couldn't touch another man without cracking some sort of embarrassed joke over it.

The first one or two times that we did this, I felt terribly self-conscious about it and didn't enjoy it, and I was really ill at ease. I guess it was about this time I visited him at his office downtown again and Monica was coming to pick me up (she had come from the printer's with my finished Ph.D. dissertation) and Larry and I had gone across the street to have a drink.

So I went out to see if she was already there, and she was. I asked her to park the car and come in. That's how it became a threesome. From then on we saw him together.

Some weeks later, after we'd seen him two or three times (just the two of us and Larry), we arrived one day and there was Paul, another psychiatrist. He said, "I want you to meet Paul, my consultant." So from then on it was a foursome. Every time we met, we met the four of us all together. Do you want to carry on from there Monica?

Shepard: How long ago was this?

Gerald: Oh, this started in November or December of sixty-eight.

Monica: Maybe a little bit later.

Shepard (to Monica): *And you got involved in seeing Larry when?*

Gerald: May of sixty-nine.

Monica: That late?

Gerald: Because it was when you picked up my dissertation.

Monica: That's right. Yeah. I remember that Jonas—our friend who recommended Larry—talked a couple of times about sitting in Larry's lap and how rewarding that was. He originally suggested to me that this psychiatrist he was seeing might be someone for Gerald to see, to help Gerald and me, to find out and understand our differences and how to live with them.

Gerald: And it was only because Jonas was a very, very good and very dear friend that I took the suggestion without being offended. If it had been anybody else. . . .

Monica: Do you want some background on me?

Shepard: Sure.

Monica: The first psychiatrist I saw was in California while I was at college. I had just broken up with Gerald in sixty-three and lots of things were going wrong with my studies and my acting and my playwriting and I decided I just had to see someone. So I went in to the psychiatric institute and they took me in as an outpatient (living out and coming in every day) and for two months I didn't go to school. I was there pretty constantly. My interest was twofold. I wanted to become a drama therapist and I was interested in working with mentally disturbed people. Also finding myself pretty disturbed at the time.

Shepard: How were you disturbed?

Monica: I was disturbed because I felt greatly rejected by Gerald. We were going through a whole thing then where he was ultrarational and I ultraemotional. It wasn't that cut and dried but that's what we were feeling. And my whole sense of femininity and my whole sense of confidence in myself as a woman was pretty shaken. And I wasn't sure where I was going or what I wanted, the kind of love that I thought I could give. I felt very unfulfilled, very dissatisfied. One of my plays that was going to be in a performance was canceled because it wasn't good enough. And I felt very bad about that. I thought it was one of the best creative works I had ever done.

So I went in and it was mostly, from what I can gather, fairly conventional psychoanalysis. It lasted for about two months, and then I went back to school and had a good summer job, finished my studies, and went up North. There I started working with a group of all teachers. It was a group encounter. We met twice a week in the evening. We were teachers interested in getting beyond our teacherness because we weren't finding our relationships with our students or the people around us very satisfying. We wanted to go in and find other ways to respond with people. We did a lot of nonverbal techniques and a lot of things which I later found out came from Esalen.

Then I moved down to Southern California and went to a group encounter there with some people I knew through college. And it was very dissatisfying because I felt that all the psychiatrists I'd been working with weren't really people. I felt them very removed. Even though they were going through good techniques and they were feeling things and I could tell they were thinking things inside, not enough seemed to come out. And then in May sixty-eight Gerald and I got married and moved East.

Shortly afterward we gave a party where I felt a lot of very, very heavy expectations of the wife role, the woman role coming down on me from Gerald. And from myself. I had to be the great hostess. This was inside of me, but I also felt it coming from Gerald and blaming him. And then Jonas mentioned this man that Gerald might go to. After a while I got very curious about what was going on in the sessions because I had a feeling from what Jonas had said that Gerald might be getting close and getting physically in contact. I knew Gerald couldn't feel that kind of warmth in a man. I've had two homosexual experiences with other women. One was very good and one was very bad. But I know what warmth there can be from someone else of the same sex and I wanted Gerald to feel that possibility too.

So when things started warming up a little bit I became very curious and I was very happy when he said, "Larry wants to meet you. Come on over."

Then there was a very tentative couple of times where Gerald and Larry and I were just feeling each other out, and Larry would say "fuck" and I would absolutely cringe and pull my vagina in and he would go a little bit further and then go still a little bit further. And after a while I found out that we relaxed one another, and Gerald and I could work together, not necessarily inhibiting each other—although sometimes we did and sometimes we didn't.

We had a couple of nude sessions: nice huggings, triangular hugs. And then when Paul came in, we kind of zapped, Paul and I. I was just very curious as to what would happen if we made love together.

I began to fantasize a lot. And I began to fantasize about Larry and about Gerald and Larry. Then we had a couple of discussions about what would happen. What would we feel, where would we be, if one or the other or both of us had sexual relations with someone else, made love with someone else or fucked someone else. And then, I really don't know how it got started. I think we were hugging and then Paul and I decided to go off into the bedroom. And it was a really very sweaty kind of animal time. I remember a lot of smells. I remember the smell of semen and his hair was very wet and he was perspiring a lot. He has a very hairy chest and that felt really nice. And he had a very short, thick cock, which [looking at Gerald] is different from yours—you have a long, big one—and it's a different body shape too because he's very heavy, overweight right now, as a matter of fact. But I liked that heaviness. Sometimes you [looking at Gerald] feel light upon me. And that was a nice difference. It felt very good.

Then we came back in the room, and I guess you and Larry must have had a wonderful scene together because you were laughing. And I remember, when we were fucking in the opposite bedroom, and you were out in the living room on some mattresses, you were laughing and we were laughing. And it was as if our laughter was blending. We could hear you way in the background and we talked about it afterward —when we were alone. What we were laughing about. And we were having a good time sharing childhood experiences about our first fucks.

Then we had another nude scene together. We had just made love that morning and we went to visit them. And we did some bioenergetics* (it was the first time we had done them—just some of the basic warm-ups), and then we started kind of rolling around on each other. And I have in my mind the image in *Morgan*, the movie, where the animals are tussling over one another. I felt that way. But I still felt a distinction between Paul and you at that time. And we made love. Oh God. I don't know how to describe that scene. It still surprises me. Gerald was inside of me. I had my . . . I don't know where, everywhere; but we were all entwined. Someone's cock was in my ear. And Paul's . . . was it Larry who was on top of you?

Gerald: Larry was sort of on the side of me and as I was fucking you . . .

Monica: But it was totally delightful.

Gerald: I had my hand on his cock and in essence jacking him off, and then we had one big orgasm all together. Paul in your ear. . . .

Monica: Did everybody come at the same time? That's nice. That's good.

Gerald: Paul in your ear, and Larry in my hand, and me in you. It was wild. That was really crazy, absolutely crazy. And at moments during that I had feelings of—no, Paul didn't come. He went later on in you.

Monica: That's right.

Gerald: But I sort of thought to myself, "Christ, conventional society would absolutely freak out if they saw or heard about this or in any way were in a position to judge." And I could sort of feel people behind my back, looking in. . . .

Monica (interrupting): Your old watcher.

Gerald: Yeah, I've got a great watcher inside of me, always watching every action I do, inhibiting me at times. Getting back to the relationship between Monica and Paul: I remember at the time, the first time this happened, I had no sense of

* Exercises developed by the followers of Wilhelm Reich.

jealousy. In fact, as Monica was saying, I was having a great
time with Larry. This was the first time that I was completely
overcoming my body fear. Larry and I were lying nude together and hugging each other and both of us had hard-ons,
but you know, that was just a nice, warm thing. And it wasn't
bothering me. I mean, I had no fear of homosexual contact or
anything like that.

And we got into some great laughter. I don't recall what
the laughter was about, but it was good and free and easy.
And it really was a release for me at that point, from my fear
of body contact with a male. And there was no sense of em-
barrassment when Monica and Paul walked in and saw us
hugging, or anything like that. But the following week, Paul
called one evening and just wanted to find out how we were
feeling about it.

Monica: Because he had had some previous bad experiences where he had fucked the wife of patients, or both of
them, and I guess he was checking up.

Gerald: I don't think that happened with a patient and a
wife, but where the husband had found out about the wife and
had a very bad reaction. But the point was that Monica talked
to Paul, and they talked for about half an hour, and then she
hung up. And at that point I felt terribly hurt and terribly let
down. Because I really felt that it was a nice relationship
between the four of us and at that point I felt that it had
become a very twosome thing between Monica and Paul, and
that's when my jealousy really reared its head and I really in a
way became crazy. And ultimately called Paul that same
night and explained to him what was happening. And we
talked for about an hour and a half or something like that. . . .

Monica: You got very angry with him. You yelled at
him.

Gerald: Yeah. I really got angry at him. Sort of like, "How
dare you speak to my wife without speaking to me?" And that
sort of thing: "If it is a togetherness relationship and you

come in with something as exclusive as that, then it becomes hurtful. Then it becomes painful." And I told of the severe mental pain that I was experiencing at this point and he understood it. And he told me about his experience that he had where he had become jealous at one time—something over his wife—where no one had screwed his wife, someone had just got friendly with her and they had shared some closeness together. Well, you know, initially that didn't sink in. But at any rate we did work it out that same night . . .

Monica: We worked on it for about two or three weeks.

Gerald: We did work most of it out that same night and then sort of got over it in meetings over the next two weeks or so. That was the only time where jealousy really entered into it, where the pain of seeing your marriage partner off in an exclusive thing with someone else was bothersome.

Monica: I think it was after that we had some good talks with Larry and Paul, where like all of us in some way or another were to be there, were to be in the scene, were to be with the others. We decided very strongly on that and kind of made it that's what we need. As a foursome. We need that. Wherever we are, whatever we're doing, everybody's going to be in on it. And that's how we continued on pretty much.

Gerald: Yeah, except when you went away on the weekend.

Monica: Yeah, but you were there.

Gerald: Why don't you relate that story?

Monica: Larry and Paul ran weekend groups and Gerald had been to one during the summer. We had decided to go separately and then go to a couples' group together later. So it was my turn to go off—it was upstate. The scene that eventually came out of the entire day, after a very long, warm sauna bath and a very, very good session all day through, was Larry and I feeling very close. I've always felt spiritually very close with him. His body doesn't attract me. He has kind of a solid force inside, which, whenever I do contact it, like I'm giving something to and getting something from.

Paul and I had had a very strong encounter earlier in the day (I don't remember whether it was nude or not) and we decided that we'd leave the group. We were going to go off and go to bed together.

And Larry said, "I wouldn't, if I were you."

He made a couple of comments about where that would leave Gerald, which was absolutely right. Paul and I had many times felt it would be great to go off and spend a week with each other. But then again, the need for other people— for Larry and Gerald being there—was very strong. Because it was a foursome. It had become a foursome in feeling and in mood and in the physicality of it and it was better to keep it that way. Maybe there was a little fear, too, that I might hurt you again [looking at Gerald], and I don't want to do that.

So Paul and I separated, and then that evening we got together again and I had gotten in Larry's bed. And as Larry and I were screwing, both of us had the tremendous sensation that Gerald was standing at the head of the bed kind of saying, "Yeah. Go. Come on. Wow."

And it felt very right. [To Gerald] I don't know where you were that Saturday night. You were away with Harvey, but I don't know where you were in feeling. But I felt you right along with us in spirit at that point.

Shepard: Why would it be all right for you and Larry to fuck without it affecting Gerald, but not for you and Paul?

Gerald: Well, I think because of the previous experience.

Monica: Because of the previous time, yeah. Also Paul was with someone else at the time, but that wouldn't affect things.

Gerald: No. I think you were afraid of going off exclusively with Paul.

Monica: Yes. Well, at the afternoon encounter I felt that way, but then I didn't want to hurt you. And I didn't feel you there. And I knew it wouldn't be good if you weren't there. I would get confused and feelings would get confused and hurt and I wanted to avoid that. But then later on with Larry, I felt you there.

Shepard (to Gerald): *How do you feel about all that?*

Gerald: Well, I accepted her explanation the way it was given. And when Larry later told me the same thing, that they really felt as though I were right there with them, I forgot about it. I said "Okay."

Monica: I had the neatest physical sensation the next morning. I had my period that morning, and I really felt all kinds of energy just coming down from my hips. Just this warm, pulsing thing kept going on, down my legs, mostly inside of my legs and from inside my hips. I didn't even know what was happening the next morning in the group. I was there, physically there, but my mind was someplace else. I felt very, very hot. Very close to an acid trip I had. At one point just this tremendous sensation of my capillaries and my ligaments and everything.

And then I felt as if I had a prick. I really for the first time could feel it very strongly and it felt very good. I could say, "That's mine." And feel the warmth of it.

I guess I must have come a couple of times. I remember having a couple of orgasms in the middle of the group, just sitting there by myself, feeling very contacted with Larry and Paul and you.

Gerald: Did you have any pot?

Monica: No. I thought of taking some, but I didn't. I had not had any drugs. And the next day Larry and I and Paul had a very warm good-bye. They were very concerned with a lot of stuff that was going on in the group, and they kind of got pulled into that.

Shepard: Where has it all led you? What has it all meant to you? Initially you went to see Larry because you felt there was a lot of friction in your marriage.

Gerald: Yeah. And that I needed to explore some of my own "woodenness"; I felt relatively wooden, or stony, in my emotions. Coming from Europe and a relatively Prussian influence of inhibiting emotions or suppressing emotions, you didn't show your emotions. All you showed was intellectual achievements, brilliance and so forth. So I had been brought up that way and I found—we found that very dissatisfying.

Monica: I guess a lot of times Larry and Paul talked about our not really being ready to meet each other yet. "You'll have to do something about yourselves first," they said. "You have to find out where you are and what you feel in it. Get some kind of contact with what's going on inside. And maybe when you do that, it will be a little bit easier." So a lot of the time we worked fairly much independently and as individuals within the foursome. And every so often we would come together, and that was very rewarding.

Gerald: In other words, one person would be working on one person's problems and the three of us would sit around and discuss that one person's problems. And then we'd come together as four.

The other interesting thing about the group relationship as it developed, and the thing which quite honestly made it easier for me to accept and continue (because in the back of my mind there was still this feeling, "I think I'm well now. Why do I continue seeing a psychiatrist?") was that we were helping each other. All four of us. And Larry and Paul expressed this many times, saying that we were as much a tonic to them, especially when we saw them on Friday evenings after a rough week. So we felt we were giving as much as we were receiving.

Shepard: Let me ask you about the business of giving and receiving. Were fees being paid at this point?

Monica: The Navy was paying them.

Gerald: Initially. In terms of paying out, I was getting free treatment. We didn't start paying until January of this year.

Shepard: But if you were helping them as much as they were helping you, why would you be paying them, rather than their paying you or having no exchange of money at all?

Gerald: This is exactly one of the feelings I had about it, you know. One of the reasons for my reluctance to start paying them was that they were getting as much out of this as they were putting in.

Monica: Yeah. Yeah.

Gerald: But she didn't agree with it.

Monica: I didn't share that. Because they called our games so many times. Both of us have games we play and I have places I put mine on. And Paul would say, "There you are. Look at yourself." And I'd go "Yeah." He would be very clear and very precise, sharing with me his experience of me and Gerald.

Shepard: Where would you put on these games?

Monica: Well, for one, anybody who's had a smattering of psychology tends to rule. I ruled it over Gerald.

Gerald: She'd psychologize.

Monica: Psychologize terribly. I still do. I'm more aware of it now.

Gerald: And you were giving me guilt complexes because I was doing things to her, or she was saying I was doing things to her, when in reality oftentimes she had put me there. Or I had allowed her to put me there by accepting her definition or her explanation. Partly because I didn't have enough psychological reading background either to . . .

Shepard (interrupting)*: to one-up her.*

Gerald: Either to one-up her or to say, "I think you're wrong."

Monica: Or to say, "That's not how I feel. You're putting me in a feeling thing."

Gerald: And I'd sort of sit there thinking maybe she's right.

Shepard: What kind of spots would she put you in?

Gerald: I think principally one of the heaviest things was the constant accusation of expectations. That *I* was putting heavy expectations on *her*. In many instances I think they were legitimate "grievances" that I had wanted to bring out and which I brought out in sort of a nagging way because I had been stymied or stifled quite often before and therefore I wouldn't be direct. Only later did I realize that she had put me there.

Shepard: So you thought it was still worthwhile to pay fees because they were doing therapeutic things for you. Were you picking up their games too?

Gerald: Oh, yeah; this is the point.

Monica: Watching them work it out was great.

Gerald: Quite oftentimes they had real problems between themselves. And we went there and in essence helped them work out their problems and then went into the car and said, "Jesus, we didn't work on anything that we had come to work on." But on the other hand, as Monica said, we learned from the way they worked their problems out.

Monica: Just watching them sit together. Sometimes we wouldn't say anything at all for a couple of hours and they would sit and have this concentrated, concentrated discussion. Back and forth. I remember the one that really affected us was their sitting and saying all the different ways they hated each other. And then they had a wrestling match. Watching that go on.

And then the other things that they would do together; I would take away and think for awhile and how I felt about it and what lessons . . . sometimes there were things in Larry like you, and in Paul like me. And sometimes we found we could learn more from the way they responded.

Shepard: Do you still see the two of them?

Gerald: Yes, but less often. Not regularly. We don't see them once a week anymore. Partly (although I guess we could again now) because the time that I was working for the Department just wasn't convenient for any of us. They couldn't see us on the weekend because they had something every weekend. We used to see them Friday nights or Saturdays for about an hour and a half or two hours. Then Monica had a lot of rehearsals on Saturday mornings. So that ruled Saturday mornings out completely. And I just couldn't leave very regularly at work.

Shepard: So the practicalities slowed it down.

Gerald: Yeah. For a while I just came in every Wednesday morning at ten o'clock to work, and from eight to nine we would see them. Then, when I had a high-pressure task to finish, we stopped.

Monica: I felt there was another reason why we stopped too. We discussed it once. And that was we had been going pretty regularly at one time and nothing much was happening. We'd done all the bioenergetics. We had had some good discussions and good feelings going on. But it seemed to be, for about a month, very stagnant. Then we went to the couples' group and that was very alive. Very in it. And we decided that we needed to change gears. And perhaps not spend our money on a weekly basis, but perhaps go once a month or so to a group.

Gerald: Not exactly once a month, but whenever a convenient group came up, we would go to those instead of meeting on a weekly basis. I think we were starting to feel that the utility level was dropping way down for the weekly sessions.

Shepard: That you had pretty much gotten what you could out of it?

Monica: We had found some ways to communicate our feelings.

Gerald: And we were feeling that we were communicating more effectively if we could use the time we spent with them

—if we used it (and this is what we planned to do although we didn't quite accomplish it)—if we used it for communicating between ourselves.

Monica: It wasn't cost-effective any more at that point. Because we had found some things that were working and we were working on them.

Shepard: Let me raise the question of how you would put it together intellectually. What the usefulness of the whole thing was. As I would recapitulate it, you, Gerald, felt wooden and emotionless and you and your wife didn't like it. You worked on that for a while. Then Monica was brought in and you got involved in all sorts of triangular, quadrangular, duangular relationships with a lot of physical involvement in every conceivable way, matter, form, shape, and whole lots of discussions about it too . . .

Gerald (Interrupting): Lots of nude hugging, too.

Shepard: Right, right. Affectionate and sexual. As you said, it was weird. Anybody listening to it would think, "Hey! A very freaky situation. Crazy people. This is terrible. It's an orgy. It meets once a week and people pay for it." So in spinning that back: what, after all this have you [looking at Gerald] felt was its usefulness as opposed to just the time you spent with Larry when you were talking with him, before everyone together became sexually ensconced.

Gerald: Well, I think one of my own lessons learned was to overcome my body fear between males. To sort of reconfirm within me that I was not a latent homosexual. That I was not a man with overt or covert homosexual tendencies, and that my want or desire to have closeness with a man was a natural thing. That it was a natural extension of my friendliness. In a sense I'm very open and affectionate. Which was until that time one of the ways I showed my emotions—by being open and affectionate.

Monica: Three-second hugging—remember we went through that—and a handshake.

Gerald: With men, yes. Because with a man-hug it was sort of phwutt, phwutt. You know? Pull, push-away sort of thing. So that was one lesson; about maleness not being impaired by that.

The lessons about sexual closeness between analysts and my wife, I don't really know whether or what kind of lessons I got out of that. I think my biggest surprise was that I was not jealous. That this could happen without causing either intense or even light jealousy. I think this was my biggest surprise about it. I don't know whether to call that a lesson.

I don't know that I would have gotten as close—emotionally and spiritually and intellectually—with both Larry and Paul had it not been for the physical closeness. I mean, if you're sitting there in your business suits, it's very nice to have an intellectual discussion about emotions and so forth and not really get anywhere. Which is what Larry and I were doing in our sessions in his office. We were just intellectualizing about my emotional problems and how they came about and what they meant in terms of childhood experiences and all that crap. Which I later came to realize was nothing more than really crap, at least in large part, I should say, because in some part it was setting a stage for Larry. It was giving him background information and I was also explaining to myself —for the first time explicitly—why I thought some things were wrong about me and what I thought the origins were. At this time Larry was doing very little analytical explanation for me or anything like that. He was simply listening and prodding me. I had to give him more.

I don't know what other lessons I drew from it. As I said, this closeness made for a greater ease of communications. Once I had gotten over this initial fear of body nudity, I think a very big barrier was sort of breached, and we could exchange almost anything.

Shepard: How has it affected relationships outside of your relationship with Larry, Paul, and your wife? For instance,

*where are you at, as a person now, that you weren't at before?
With people in general?*

Gerald: It's very very difficult working in the Department
to have experiences like that affect your business life. But with
some very dear friends we developed something similar, a
close intimacy. It wasn't where we were cross-fucking each
other or anything like that. It's just that we had nice hugs
and nice togetherness evenings. We were being together just
by being together.

In terms of my relationship with Monica, this is very definitely changed, because we can now communicate. In the
release of inhibitions that came about with the overcoming of
the body nudity thing (especially since we did it together),
there was a great deal of improvement in our way of communicating together.

*Shepard: Did either of you have any sexual problem before
the thing began? Aversions, discomforts, potency problems,
satisfactional problems?*

Gerald: I don't consider having had problems, but I think
you thought I had a cleanliness fetish.

Monica: Yeah. I think we have different attitudes about
body odors. Since then, I've felt it's just easier all the way
around to experiment with different positions and different
ways of doing things. A little bit easier for you to sweat, for
you perhaps to enjoy my odors, even though I still have to
clean myself very strongly.

Gerald: Well, you know, you're an actress. And if you
don't clean yourself, you stink.

Monica: That's very simple. That's very true at times.

Shepard (to Monica): *How about you? I get an impression
as we talk about it that you always thought you were kind of a
loose chick and into things and emotions, and your husband
was the stiff one, the cardboard one. And now that he's looser
you can do your thing together rather than take his trips together, or something like that.*

Monica: It's an easy bag to fall into because I like to see myself like that. It's an image that I very consciously perpetrated on many people. But I've learned in many ways that I'm just not as loose and free as I'd like to think myself to be. That I have a lot of tightnesses. I found that I have a great big watcher inside of me, too, that never even contacted me before.

It's hard for me to intellectualize about my feelings and my changes and everything else. It's much easier for me to say "Ah, yeah. Wow! Great. Good scene," and leave it at that. I realize now that is very easy for me to do. It's hard for me to sit down and think what coherent lessons, messages, analysis can I make of my experiences that help me and help us go somewhere.

Shepard: What do you think was the usefulness of all the fucking, hugging, touching? [To Gerald] *Did you and Larry screw at some point?*

Gerald: No.

Shepard: You were just hugging and at one point jerked him off?

Gerald: Yes. The jacking off was only that one time when we were all in that foursome.

Monica: Since I was sixteen and I had my first sexual relations I'd always felt, "What am I going to do when I marry someone, if I marry someone, and it's exclusive and it's one person? And how am I going to share with him all my other experiences?" As a teen-ager, Gerald was the second man I went to bed with. Then we separated and came together again. And we shared nothing at that point. I was afraid to tell him that I had had someone before him. But in between that time I screwed around a lot and had a lot of bad screws. I found out I was using sex as a substitute for intimacy, for closeness, for communication between people. And not as the bond it can be.

Well, I thought, "When I get married, what am I going to

do? How am I going to tell the man that I marry about all these past things?" Because they're very much a part of where I am now. They've helped me become "me" now. And I guess I had a great deal of curiosity as to whether monogamy would work. What different kinds of love can two married people have with themselves, with each other and with other people? Because I feel I could love a lot of people, I could marry a lot of people.

Gerald: But that was part of your over-confidence.

Monica: Yeah. That was the professional open cunt. Whenever I would go into a group I would put myself into that role of the professional open cunt. The warm earth mother. "Come to me and you can suck my tits anytime," you know. Being very open to everybody, but yet not learning that at the same time I was *closed* open; I was *shut* open. I was stuck open. But it wasn't openness out of choice. And this is something that I ran into with a lot of people at Esalen, and I would say, "Oh boy. They're really stuck open."

There's choice in sharing and there's choice in pulling away. Some people like me feel that there's some kind of communion going on just glancing and looking and whatever and feel the choice, feel the freedom to say, "No. It's great. We have a good thing going here but I'm really into something now with my husband." That's what I told one of my teachers: "We could go into something but right now, but I'd rather say no than have myself and my image of myself being pushed into . . ."

Gerald (interrupting): a leaky tit situation where you just did it to help him?

Monica: No. That would be you! But that I would enjoy seeing myself in that role with him.

Gerald: Okay. What was your "stuck openness?"

Monica: Well, that requires a little bit of history. I was a very sickly child. Also as a child and a young teen-ager I looked very innocent, very pure. An angelic quality. Lots of people told me this. And to prove to people that I was not such an innocent, I would carry around a little bag of tricks, gross tricks. Like saying "fuck" when I knew it would just make someone piss, and I was really enjoying it. Because my parents always held me as being such an innocent. And I wanted to prove to everyone that I was real, that I was evil, that I was down, that I was up, that I was bright and that there was a lot inside of me. That I wasn't just that simple. So I would carry around experiences and pop them on people.

Shepard (to Monica): *What did Larry and Paul do for you compared to other therapists you've seen?*

Monica: They were all there. They were people. When they were confused or frustrated or irritated at me, when they really liked me, when they felt that I was doing something awful or that I was saying something inauthentic, they'd let me know. And then they would make me think about it. Also they were able to say—like if I needed someone to hug me— they would say, "Listen, I can't hug you right now, I'm somewhere else."

Like Larry would be worried about his children or be very upset that he wouldn't be able to be with them in some way. And then I'd come on and want to be with him and then he'd say, "Look. I just can't be there, I'd be pretending if I try to be with you now." And that kind of made me begin to experiment. Maybe I'm really fooling myself to say that I can be with everyone, or a man, all the time. Sometimes I need to be able to say (if my feelings warrant it), "I'm distraught. I'm angry, I'm tired, or I'm somewhere else." And to say that, to say to myself, "I'm unavailable for you right now."

Gerald: In other words, you started to recognize the fallaciousness of your openness, and the falseness of it sometimes [Monica murmurs her assent] and that's one of the helpful things.

Shepard: Do you think that your marriage is in better shape now?

Gerald: Oh, yeah. Very definitely.

Shepard: Do you plan on having any children?

Gerald: Maybe.

Monica: Sometimes. Sometimes we do and sometimes we don't.

Shepard: How have you managed to deal with the question of fidelity in marriage? How about fucking outside the quadrangle.

Monica: It's been odd.

Gerald: Because the first time it happened, it happened sort of connected to the context of the quadrangle. What happened was that it was at a party that Larry and Paul—or Paul gave—and there was another couple there (well, there were several couples there) plus Paul's sister. I got very friendly with Paul's sister and we thought it would be nice to just fuck. So we went up to the bedroom and just fucked. At the same time, I could see that in the front of the room, Monica was getting into something with some guy. So I didn't think it was necessary to ask permission . . .

Monica (interrupting): To check . . .

Gerald (continuing): . . . to check each others' feelings because we were both sort of at the same place.

Monica: And I turned around to see—to check—with Gerald. Because I had been dancing with this guy and we wanted to screw, and God, Gerald was already off in the bedroom. So I thought, I like Paul's sister. I really do like her. I'm glad it was . . . what I'm thinking right now is that it's pretty damn silly to think that one person can be all for another person. Remember the movie we saw? *Women in Love?* Where the one woman toward the end could not understand that she could not be everything for her husband? I feel that strongly, that I cannot be everything to you. That's why I understand Ruthie—[to Shepard] someone from work that he went to bed with—because she can share a lot with you that I am not interested in, don't necessarily enjoy discussing.

So when you have these half-hour-long discussions on the telephone with her, I'm glad. I feel a lot of animation in your discussion. And that's something about politics that I can't share.

Gerald: We both have a sense that infidelity is all right only if it's understood by the other person. Jealousy has never been a problem in our relationship.

Shepard: Are you really that cool about it? You don't get up-tight about it at all?

Monica: The only time it really upset me was after I went to a weekend myself and came home Sunday evening. I thought that Gerald was going to be there, but he left a note that he was out of town with Harvey, a friend of ours. And all of a sudden I felt, you ought to be here with me. Waiting for me so that I could share with you my marvelous experiences. And you weren't there. Now I didn't know—to me you were just off—but good things were happening with you.

Gerald: Harvey and I slept with each other that night when we were away, and it was sort of my first homosexual experience other than Larry and Paul (whom I consider as having taken me past a barrier) and it was a weird feeling.

Shepard: Weird, how?

Gerald: Weird in the sense that I wasn't afraid of it. I felt that we were sharing an instance . . . Harvey and I had been friends from about a month and a half after I arrived in the East. We had very intellectual discussions. I had stayed overnight at his apartment house, but you know, nothing intimate. No touch or anything like that. And we went away that time, and we slept in the same bed. It's funny but that was all that was available at the hotel.

Shepard: It wasn't planned, you mean?

Gerald: I don't know whether it was planned on his part or not, but it wasn't planned on my part. And Harvey at that point confessed to always having had a great love for me. And I remember not feeling uncomfortable about that. And when he turned toward me and he hugged me, we then took off our pajamas, and hugged each other and fondled each others' genitals, and that was about it. And I remember it as being a pleasant sensation and my not having any guilt feelings about it. I suppose in retrospect I feel a bit weird about it—surprised in a sense that it happened. And still not knowing for certain how to evaluate it. In other words, in the back of my mind there's still this tiny flicker of, "Oh, that was wrong." And . . . well, at any rate, that was it.

Shepard: Talking about it, too, it sounds as though if it weren't conceptualized, if the act had absolutely no symbolic meaning, it would just be part of the flow of whatever your daily life was, like shaking hands or this or that. But somehow conceiving of it or labeling it as something homosexual bothered you more than anything that transpired between you.

Gerald: That's exactly it. What transpired between us, doesn't bother me. But the label that might be put on it by someone square, by some fucking security investigator who might find out about that and thereby ruin any vision of public life later on, that's what bothers me. My own attitudes, I feel, are very open. But the watcher that sees everything in terms of how society would look at this, says, "Geez, you'd better watch that. Because if you don't and you're found out, there goes your life down the drain."

Shepard: What were the best and what were the worst things of Larry's and Paul's kind of treatment?

Gerald: I can't think of anything negative right now.

Monica: Can I answer that? One of the fears that both of us share is that we somehow won't be able to sustain a marriage, a close relationship, for some time. And one of the better things that I can think of is that they have enabled both of us to realize that there's a little bit more chance of sustaining it. My sister's been divorced three times, my parents had very little closeness, and I've known very little closeness in my life. A lot of fucking, but not much intimacy in it. And we're going on our second year now, and the four of us feel that to be a real good accomplishment. And through them we felt a little bit more competent . . .

Gerald: Of being able to work on problems . . .

Monica: . . . by ourselves. In many ways we're mismatched, but maybe we can learn from each other. And . .

Gerald: What do you mean mismatched? [both laugh]

Monica: You know what I mean.

Gerald: I know. Well, we have completely different professional interests. She's in the theater and I'm interested in politics and law. I've had little, if any, contact with psychology. The only book in that field I read was Erich Fromm's *The Art of Loving,* and that seemed at the time the ultimate truth. Furthermore, Monica had a strong aversion to even reading the news, so in that sense our intellectual interests just didn't coincide. One of the things that we found with Larry and Paul was that we had a number of things that held us together and that it could be mutually beneficial and that . . .

Monica: I love you.

Gerald: Yeah. And that we were pretty damn good for each other and . . .

Monica: . . . and that it feels nice to love. And to like.

Gerald: Yeah. And the important thing was that the love of the other person was helping each of us realize more of ourselves. We felt a hell of a lot better for having been married than we were when we were single.

Monica: Larry said something that really hit for a while and I'm just coming back to it again: "If you can find the woman inside of Gerald and the man inside yourself, you can be people touching each other and not husband and wife." It was one of his pontifications, I'm sure. It sounds that way. But it was said with a lot of concern and a lot of warmth. And it comes back.

Shepard: What do you think therapy is, or should be, about?

Monica: I think it's pretty damn easy in this society to get disaffected and disconnected and to lose contact with yourself —with what's going on at the moment, what's happened in the past and your feelings about it. I feel very strongly about that. In my work, with the people I'm in contact with, they really seem concerned with lots of things that don't concern me. When I meet people that are concerned with the same things that I'm concerned with, it's a pleasant surprise and shock and a new world to discover, a new place to be. Therapy does that for me and I think it should do that for people.

Gerald: I think, basically, also that it's so easy to screw up our self-image in today's world. Partly from the expectations that are put on us at work. Partly from the role we play at work, and we carry that home. I think it affects life at home if you don't openly discuss it and bring it out. And I feel that most people are not equipped analytically to be aware, to discuss and cope with this distortion of their own image, because of what they're doing. For me therapy is putting me in touch with some of these false images I built up about myself, letting me see through them to cope with them, to try to establish the real me.

Shepard: I would think today that another aspect of it would be making available to people, ideally, every conceivable possibility, every conceivable experience without injuring them or doing them damage, but making them open to almost any way of existence.

Gerald: I would agree.

AUTHOR'S POSTSCRIPT

While the sexual activities of Monica, Gerald, Paul, and Larry might well offend the average reader, one would be hard put to find any ill effect therefrom. Indeed, they seemingly helped Gerald to have friendlier relationships with men (unencumbered by fear of homosexuality), and allowed both Gerald and Monica to deal with the question of fidelity in marriage. That issue is one that must be resolved in every marriage, and here it seems to have taken place under fairly well-controlled circumstances.

In addition, the problem that brought them into therapy, seems to have been satisfactorily resolved. The marriage stabilized, the blaming game ended, and they appear to take a great deal of pleasure in their relationship with each other.

On balance, the therapeutic experience was a good one. Monica seems to have been helped primarily by the nonsexual aspects of treatment—Paul's skillfullness in catching on to her games and by the honest expressions of feelings both Larry and Paul displayed. For her, the sexual relationships with Larry and Paul did not, apparently, alienate her affection for Gerald.

For Gerald, the male-to-male intimacies were an essential ingredient of the positiveness of therapy. Paradoxically, but understandably, the fact that he was brought to the point of being able to have a homosexual relationship, both freed him from the fear of and desire for homosexuality. And, as has been mentioned, it led to his shedding his uncomfortably arch formality in the company of other men.

Could this couple have been helped by more conventional therapists? Gerald says "No," and in view of both his and Monica's previous bouts with conventional psychotherapists, one would be hard pressed to argue with them. Are Larry and Paul "kooks" for wrestling and fighting with one another while taking fees from Gerald? Their actions seem less bizarre when one realizes that such ways of relating are standard procedure in many successful encounter groups which stress that everyone—including the therapist—is to express honestly his feelings both in word and action. And Larry and Paul, while trained as psychiatrists and, in Larry's case, psychoanalysis, both seem to have had extensive encounter experience.

Suppose the therapists got as much as they gave. Why,

then, pay them a fee? Monica supplied some justification for that. When it was no longer cost-effective, they stopped treatment. Gerald and Monica were nobody's dupes. They employed some unconventional therapists to help them resolve some very conventional problems.

14

CONCLUSIONS AND GUIDELINES FOR PATIENTS AND THERAPISTS

One is somewhat hesitant to write that a sexual involvement can be a useful part of the psychotherapeutic process. How could the author conclude so much on the basis of a series of two-hour interviews? Aren't some of the patients' endorsements of intimacy possibly self-defensive excuses and rationalizations?

These are fair questions. One of the reasons I presented the material as I did—as personal accounts rather than as my *interpretations* of these accounts—was to permit the patient-participant in the intimacy to speak directly to the reader, who was free to determine by himself (without the author's editorializing) the degree of honesty, fullness, and perspective of these accounts. And while it is true that endorsements of intimacy can be the result of self-defensive rationalizations, it is equally true that attacks on intimacy may also spring from the same source.

Just as the author had to make up his own mind about the usefulness of the intimacies reported in these cases, just as he had to struggle to make some interpretive sense of what it all meant, so will each reader have to do likewise. I no more desire to treat the reader as a "child," than I do a patient. As I said at the outset, I regard this book as an initial attempt to provoke serious discussion and argument about a heretofore secret, arbitrarily damned, and yet not uncommon practice.

Still, I would like to share with the reader some of my own conclusions, tentative though some of them may be.

It seems to me that any open-minded listening to what these eleven patient-participants have had to say must lead to the conclusion that intimacy with a therapist can indeed be useful. In my opinion, Beverly (the Midwestern editor whose account began this book; who had a seven year affair with an essentially impotent psychoanalyst); Kathy (the twenty-three-year-old case worker, whose intimacy with Jason, the man who led a marathon session she attended, led her to feel very desirable and beautiful); Jessie (the poised and professional West coast Ph.D. candidate in psychology, who had a friendly and professionally worthwhile affair with a former therapist); Gerald and Monica (the couple whose account of intimacy with two male co-therapists completes the body of this book), and Nicholas (who had a homosexual affair with Ralph), all had useful experiences because they were intimate with their therapists.

My reluctance to write that a sexual involvement can be helpful arises because of the equal possibility that intimacy can be harmful, as it was with Marcus (the student who was led into a bizarre series of misadventures by Susan, his nearly fifty-year-old professor and later therapist at college); with Bonnie (the baker of hashish brownies for the sexually sadistic George); and with Judy (the promiscuous thief who fought fiercely with her parents and felt betrayed by her intimacy with a therapist who was also her brother's friend). And because it is equally possible that intimacy with one's therapist can simply be a diversionary waste of time—as with Carol (the voluptuary with a false pregnancy, whose therapist couldn't get rid of her) and Barbara (the remote and depressed cellist who felt she had to be perfect).

In addition, the instability of many therapists makes me reluctant to do anything or state anything that would encourage them toward closer contact with their patients. Aside from their general personality quirks, some of the therapists mentioned by those I interviewed obviously had sexual problems of a far greater magnitude than the people whom they were treating. This was quite clear in the reports of both Beverly and Bonnie.

Yet I do not want to spend any great amount of time speculating on the therapist's personality or sexual problems. For one thing, it would be unfair and arbitrary. These interviews were conducted with patients—not with therapists. Therefore, my data on the therapists is inadequate, to say the least. Nor do I want to speculate or pontificate about a therapist's powers of persuasion; about his powers to manipulate the therapeutic situation so as to bed his patients. Certainly, patients are far more open to the suggestions of a therapist than they would be to those of the man on the street, and certainly any therapist should be aware of this power and should offer suggestions to the patient that are likely to be in the *patient's* best interest. Yet let us not assume that a patient's need for a sexual experience and a therapist's desire might not coincide. For they well may. Neither should it be presumed that a twentieth-century psychotherapist can play Svengali to his patient's Trilby. Such powers disappeared, for all intents and purposes, generations ago.

Rather than place myself in the sterile bind of being either a proponent or abolitionist of intimacy in the psychotherapeutic situation, I prefer simply to say, "It's there. It exists. What can we learn from it so as to minimize its hazards and maximize its assets?"

Damning it is no more likely to lead to its disappearance than the damning of drugs, adultery, or ungodliness has led to the vanishing of those phenomena. Damnation will only increase both participants' shame, guilt, and furtiveness. Praising the practice might lead to such excesses that many more meaningless or hazardous involvements would ensue. Some momentary pleasure, perhaps. But one needn't spend upward of twenty-five dollars an hour in a therapist's office if one's primary aim is merely to find a lover.

The accounts that have been presented here detail actual experiences of therapist-patient intimacies. They are not intended to serve as models. Several of them, on the contrary, should serve as models of avoidance. Even in those instances where the patient avers having benefited, it is clear that some of the therapists stumbled into the intimacy without a clear purpose in mind, and, once involved, did not know how to guide it to its proper end.

This is not surprising. There are no reputable therapeutic training centers that deal with the subject except in a completely prohibitive way. There are no formal texts with case histories that show how psychotherapeutic intimacies have been handled successfully, as there are, for instance, books detailing successful treatments of schizophrenia. In a sense, we are only at the beginning of dealing with the issue, and much of what we have to work with is based on fragmentary information. But even the most abject failure can be of use in establishing guidelines and criteria, even if only negative ones, and the most modest success can be a guide to the light.

For me, psychotherapy is in its ultimate sense an educative process. It contains the potential to help people become aware of their own feelings, and it can teach them more about how they and other people interact. No more and no less.

People who feel at ease rarely go to see a therapist. Those who do go feel troubled. Their minds are preoccupied. They are locked into interactions with other people that spark a great deal of anguish within themselves and they have an insufficient awareness to gain much perspective on how they themselves helped bring the situation about. They feel trapped in their patterns and long to be free. Their options in dealing with others are limited to the degree that finding a way out seems improbable to them. Neither do they have the perspective not to take certain problems seriously.

Both Marcus and Carol raise the question of *what is psychotherapy*? Is it therapy for the mind—relief of anguish? Or is it the broadening of experience—learning more about how the world functions and how one can live in it ably? For me, it is both. Although new experiences will at times cause some anguish for reason of their very *newness*, when psychotherapy is effective the person undergoing it will feel a steady decline of his level of anxiety.

If psychotherapy is educative, then patients are not "sick." Rather, they are unknowledgeable about some important—perhaps crucial—facets of their own psychology. Indeed, *patient* is a grossly inaccurate term—a holdover from medical training and social usage. *Student* would be a more apt term, because hopefully the therapist has something to teach him about human psychology and social interactions. To call the lack of awareness "sickness" must either stamp us all as sick or encourage the manipulations that certain poorly aware people use to deny their responsibility. Their argument goes like this: "Take care of me. I'm sick. And if things go wrong, it's *your* fault because I'm neurotic."

No less than any other social interaction, sex is susceptible to improvement through teaching. Ideally, the homosexual can be taught that relating to a woman will not destroy him; the frigid woman can be taught to face the unreal fears she has of male penetration; the lesbian can be taught what it is like to experience a man's affection. And much of this teaching may be accomplished through intimacy that is handled by the therapist with tact, judgment, sensitivity and a deep understanding of his patient and his patient's goals.

For the therapist, four *rules* for intimacy are suggested by the cases presented in the earlier chapters.

1. *He must not be too "needy" of his patient, either sexually or emotionally.* It was the exceptional possessiveness of Marcus's therapist and the unselective sexual neediness of Judy's therapist that were largely instrumental in leading to their destructive interactions. The best protection against such needfulness occurs when the therapist in his private life has a meaningful and satisfying sex-love life. Nicholas' treatment, which was spectacularly successful, occurred with a therapist who was apparently satisfactorily married and had another meaningful homosexual relationship. Indeed, the one disappointing transaction that occurred between Nicholas and his therapist, Ralph, took place when Ralph's wife and family were away and he had a falling out with Earl, his homosexual friend. This increased Ralph's needfulness and led to his pulling Nicholas toward him at a time when allowing him to break free was indicated.

2. *He must be prepared to discuss the intimacy with the patient.* The great failure (by which I mean the enormously wasteful, as opposed to harmful, effect) of Barbara's therapy is attributable to the failure of either person to bring up for discussion the most significant event in their relationship. While lovers may take their intimacy for granted, a therapist who does so abdicates his role as a healer-teacher. He is there to help bring meaning and awareness to his patient-student's chaos and amorphousness. The patient's expectations, wishes, fantasies, and demands, made as a lover, are a rich ground indeed for psychotherapeutic exploration. An intimate therapist should be an adult and responsible therapist, one able to focus on the significance of the involvement.

Beverly's experience, while useful over a protracted period of time, could have been foreshortened and made more valid if her therapist-lover had brought up for discussion his own inadequacies as a lover and solicited her response to this. He might also have questioned her as to why she continued to see him so tenaciously when he was no great shakes as a lover and did not intend to leave his wife. Here, too, it is probable that his needfulness for her might have prevented him from helping her to get the message, "You can't always get what you want," earlier.

In contrast, the success of Nicholas's and Gerald's treatment can be attributed in large measure not only to their therapists' willingness to involve themselves sexually, but to thoroughly discuss their involvements as well.

3. *He must not become sexually involved with someone where intimacy would repeat a previously bad pattern.* Sexual intimacy worked best in those instances where it provided an opportunity to act out a new and previously feared (though desired) relationship—as in the cases of Nicholas, Gerald, and, to an extent, Kathy. It was disastrous with Judy, whose casual attitude toward sex filled her with self-loathing.

This repetition of a bad pattern was also responsible for the destructiveness of Bonnie's involvement. It was not the casualness of intimacy that was harmful here, because Bonnie did not view her sexual openness as a bad thing, but rather her self-concept when dealing with impotent men.

4. *Being available is one thing; being insistent is another.* A therapist's ultimate responsibility is to "be there," able to accommodate himself to his patient-student's flow of feelings and able to detach himself sufficiently so as to further the understanding of that flow. He is not paid a fee to impose his flow upon his clients.

Bonnie's therapist insisted on imposing his mechanistic, sadistic sexual "trip" upon her even though she was not interested in it. Judy's therapist insisted, apparently, on imposing his flow on every attractive girl who entered his office. Marcus's therapist in some ways did the same.

In all instances where good results obtained, the therapist went no further than his client's own interests.

Guidelines for the client suggest themselves as well:

1. *He should consider himself a client or student instead of a patient*. This means giving up certain rights and privileges of the "emotionally ill." It means assuming responsibility for the intimacy, too, and not hiding behind the myth of helplessness, neurosis, and the argument, "It's all his fault for taking advantage of a poor sickie like me."

Barbara failed to do this and so her experience was, psychotherapeutically speaking, meaningless. Judy, in spite of having had a disturbed therapist, failed to see herself as an active participant in the intimacy and thus abdicated responsibility. She apparently preferred to see herself as a helpless object, maltreated by parents and by a therapist whom she could blame for her troubles.

While it is true that a good therapist would never knowingly participate in a destructive relationship, sexual or nonsexual, it is equally true that therapists, being human, are subject to blind spots. Barbara's therapist might well have done a better job with her if she had told him what she felt and thought, instead of irresponsibly and silently waiting around to be "done" to. Further, blind faith in a therapist on the patient's part is as unrealistic as blind faith in one's parents. Marcus, Bonnie, and, to a lesser degree, Judy, trusted too readily. Basic mistrust is as necessary a part of our equipment as is basic trust and faith. If you are old enough to be intimate, be old enough to assume responsibility for the intimacy.

2. *He should be leery of any therapist who becomes possessive*. When a client starts to feel in an intimate relationship with a therapist, that he is being held on to, then he must talk about it. The therapist's possessiveness can subtly manifest itself in such a way that the patient may begin to feel that he can't discuss his involvements with other people, that he

must acquiesce to the therapist's sexual or social desires, or that he can't tell him things that might hurt his feelings. On the other hand, these fears may only be based on illusory presumptions.

A therapist who allows himself to be intimate should be able to deal with such misgivings. If the client can't get past them after talking about them, he'd be better off switching therapists. His goal is to find freedom, not another master.

3. *He should be responsible for bringing up at all times reactions, secret wishes, doubts, and feelings relating to the therapist.* His goal in therapy is not to protect the therapist's ego, but to develop his own. Beverly's failure to recognize this made her involvement less constructive than it might have been. The same is true for Barbara. Bonnie's candid rejection of her therapist's impotence freed her to pursue more satisfying relationships.

These feelings should also be explored even before the intimacy begins, as occurred with Nicholas and Gerald and Monica.

4. *If he is suffering more than he was before the intimacy began, he should break off the relationship.* The patient came to see a therapist to relieve turmoil, not increase it. Marcus particularly prolonged his anguish by continuing in the intimacy longer than he should have. At least Judy had the sense to break it off.

In summation, I would say that these cases indicate that as many people are aided by intimate involvements with their therapists as are hurt, and no blanket prejudgments concerning the ethicalness or validity of intimacy per se ought to be made.

If the therapist's ultimate responsibility is to help his patient grow and learn, any and all means should be valid in reaching this goal. I doubt that any conventionally "ethical" therapist could have helped Nicholas as much as Ralph did. For me, a violation of ethics occurs when the therapist fails to help a person grow and learn when certain actions or restraints on the therapist's part would clearly have been useful. Thus, I lack ethics because I did not respond more honestly to my lesbian patient—the adolescent whom I encountered during my training. And both Judy's and Bonnie's therapists lacked ethics for not restraining themselves.

If sexual involvement occurs it ought to be selective, meaningful, and honest. I suspect that owing to the possessiveness, confusion of roles, guilt, and shame *on the part of most therapists*, such involvement is, generally speaking, not a good idea. To become intimately involved, a therapist must not only be comfortable and free with his own sexuality, but be a decent, respectful, and independent human being besides.